D1368509

Presented to

by

Mommow & Poppaw Hartman

on

July 16 2004

MY GOOD NIGHT PRAYERS

45
Quiet Times with Prayers, Songs, & Rhymes

written by Susan L. Lingo
illustrated by Kathy Parks

Standard
PUBLISHING
CINCINNATI, OHIO

© 2002 Susan L. Lingo. © 2002 Standard Publishing, Cincinnati, Ohio. A division of Standex International Corporation. All rights reserved. Sprout logo is a trademark of Standard Publishing. My Good Night® is a registered trademark of Standard Publishing. Printed in Italy. Project editor: Robin M. Stanley. Cover design: Robert Glover. Art direction: Coleen Davis. Graphic arts: Dina Sorn.

Scriptures quoted from the *International Children's Bible®, New Century Version®*, copyright © 1986, 1988, 1999 by Tommy Nelson™, a division of Thomas Nelson, Inc., Nashville, Tennessee 37214. Used by permission.

08 07 06 05 04 03 02   9 8 7 6 5 4 3

Library of Congress Cataloging-in-Publication Data

Lingo, Susan L.
    My good night prayers : 45 quiet times with prayers, songs & rhymes / written by Susan
L. Lingo ; illustrated by Kathy Parks.
        p. cm.
    Includes index.
    Summary: Presents Bible stories and verses, prayers, songs, and activities to be shared
in quiet times on such topics as creation, trust, obedience, and thankfulness.
    ISBN 0-7847-1365-0 (hard cover)
    1. Prayers—Juvenile literature. 2. Bedtime—Juvenile literature. 3.
Children—Prayer-books and devotions. [1. Prayer books and devotions.] I. Parks, Kathy
(Kathleen D.), ill. II. Title.

BV4870 .L543 2002
242'.62—dc21
                                                                2002022539

from Susan

To my darling father, Warren, through whom I was embraced by the warmth of prayer. And to my Heavenly Father, through whom I have experienced the power of prayer!

"God does nothing but by prayer, and everything with it." —John Wesley

from Kathy

With thanks to God for inspiring us all, every tick of the clock.

Contents

New Testament

Dear Parents and Caregivers,

The lives of children (and grown-ups) are busy, busy, busy! There are so many places to go, people to know, and ways to grow. Sometimes it's hard to find peaceful moments to share together and quiet times to be with God. Though these opportunities may be the toughest to find, they can be the most important times you share, especially in those precious early years of your child's life. *My Good Night® Prayers* will help you and your child discover the joys of quiet time with God, and will help you draw closer to each other and God through peaceful prayers, happy praises, and God's Word. What a wonderful way to share precious moments with your child!

Why is quiet time important?

Children spend most of their days hurrying and scurrying from one exciting activity to another. After all, there is so much to learn and experience in their bright, new worlds! But too much activity and stimulation can be overwhelming to young children. Just as harried and hurried grown-ups need a bit of peace and quiet during busy days, children need time to rest, relax, and refocus their attention. Whether it's in the middle of the day or at bedtime, quiet times give your child physical as well as emotional rest and refreshment and allow him to be still and thoughtful before God. Planned quiet times offer the best way for your child to stop, take a breath, and interact with the ones he loves most—you and God!

What you can do to teach your child to pray.

Praying isn't an innate ability; rather, it's a learned expression. Just as Jesus' disciples learned how to pray from Jesus (Luke 11:1), children need to be taught about prayer in gentle, loving ways. Here are a few suggestions for teaching and enriching your child's prayer life:

- Provide quiet times to talk with God during the day, not just at bedtime.
- Act as a role model in allowing your child to see you praying and spending quiet time with God.
- Assure your child that God hears every prayer we pray because he loves us. Explain that because God loves us, he promises to answer our prayers in his own time and way.
- Work Scripture into prayer time

whenever possible! Scripture teaches God's truths and provides a marvelous base for prayers. For example, you might base a simple prayer on Psalm 118:24 and pray, "This is the day that the Lord has made and we are glad. Thank you for this day, God. Amen."

- Look for and recognize God's special gifts throughout the day and nurture your child's natural desire to tell God "thank you" for his gifts.

How can this book help?

If you've read *My Good Night® Bible* and *My Good Night® Devotions,* then you've already met our favorite firefly friend, Night-Light! Now snuggle up as Night-Light helps your child to know God's Word, delight in God's joyous gifts, and offer thanks through gentle prayers and happy praises. Each section of *My Good Night® Prayers* offers quiet time activities while learning God's truths and offering loving thanks and praise.

Knowing God's Word helps young children recognize and appreciate God's power and truth, and challenges them to read a Bible verse all by themselves! *Enjoying God's Gifts* contains fun rhymes and songs and play-alongs so you can teach children about the glorious gifts God brings us every day. And *Giving God Thanks* centers around a prayerful, joyous expression of thanks to our heavenly Father. With Night-Light beside them and you to guide them, your children will express their feelings and thanks to God through prayer. In addition, they will begin to recognize God's gifts, and feel love for our Lord who freely helps, heals, and provides for us!

Together-time tips for bedtime or anytime

- Relax! Set aside the worries and duties of the day, slow down and just be with your child. Observe how many minutes it takes your child to become still and more focused. Be sure to allow enough "settling down" time—for both of you!

- The stories, devotions, and prayers included in all three *My Good Night®* books are made to accompany each other in order of their appearance in each book. For example, story number one in *My Good Night® Bible* matches the theme of story number one in *My Good Night® Devotions* and prayer time number one in *My Good Night® Prayers*. If you use *My Good Night® Bible* and *My Good Night® Devotions* along with *My Good Night® Prayers,* consider reading one story for nap time and the accompanying ones for bedtime or as a wonderful review the next day. Invite your child to retell the previous Bible story or devotion before reading the matching prayer time pages.

- Match your prayer times with real-life situations your child may be experiencing. If your child needs a gentle reminder about obeying, read the prayer time entitled *Always Obey* (page 29). Remember that sincere prayers reflect our thoughts and emotions—not just words we've memorized!

- Invite your child to a "prayer share" party. Have cookies or crackers and juice as you talk about why God loves for us to talk with him. Remind your child that God hears every one of our prayers. Then create your own prayer poster by letting your child dictate a simple prayer thanking God for listening to us. (Limit your prayer to four lines so it will be easy to learn.) Work with your child to decorate the edges of the poster with colorful pictures and designs. Then repeat your prayer every day until you both know it by heart!

- Enjoy the precious prayers and praises in *My Good Night® Prayers* at bedtime, nap time—anytime you and your child want to experience the fullness of God's truths and express to him the joy of your love!

Prayer Time Rhyme

Come, let's share a prayer,
a prayer, a prayer—
Come, let's share a prayer
and talk to our Lord.
To say, "God, I love you,"
And tell God "I thank you;"
Oh, come, let's share a prayer
and talk to our Lord.

Slumber Song

(to the tune of "Jesus Loves Me")

Let's tuck you in, turn off the light—
now it's time to say "Good night."
God is watching over you,
he keeps us safe the
whole night through.
Chorus:
God's love is near us,
God's love is near us,
God's love is near us,
sleep tight, I love you, dear.

I go to bed
and sleep in peace.
Lord, only you keep me safe.

Psalm 4:8

Hi, I'm Night-Light,
your special firefly friend!

Come with me as I help you to remember some of my favorite Bible stories. Then we will spend quiet time together with God. We'll pray to him and praise him, too—thanking him for all the neat things he does! My ladybug pal will always be somewhere in every Bible story picture. Be sure to look for her! Let's get started!

Who made the world such a special place to be?
What do you enjoy about God's creation?

God Made the World

God said, "I made the earth." Isaiah 45:12

Knowing God's Word . . . a story to read

Who made the world? God made the world. God made the
world a nice place to be and added such beauty for you and for
me! Only God is wise enough and powerful enough to make a
whole world. Only God is our Creator. And what a wonderful
world God made for us: flowers, birds, and bees that buzz;
oceans and stars and dandelion fuzz. What a wonderful world!

When God made the world, he added many special touches.
God added colors like red, blue, green, and yellow. Can you find
all the yellow flowers and the orange caterpillar? God added
shapes like triangles, circles, and squares. Then God added
something very wonderful to the world. God added love! Only
God can make a world and only God can add his love! How do
we know? The Bible tells us so!

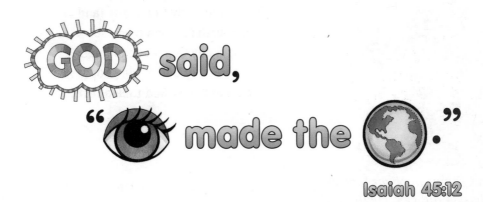

GOD said, "👁 made the 🌍."

Isaiah 45:12

21

Enjoying God's Gifts . . . a song to sing

God made the world. God made the world in seven days. Can you count to seven? 1, 2, 3, 4, 5, 6, 7! Each day God made special gifts to hear and see—special gifts for you and me. And God saw that it was good. Let's sing a special song about all the gifts God gave us on every day he created.

CREATION SONG
(tune: *Old McDonald*)

On the first day God made light—
Thank you, thank you, Lord!
God made light and it was good—
Thank you, thank you, Lord!

With light, light here, and light, light there—
Here is light, there is light, everywhere is light, light!
On the first day God made light—
Thank you, thank you, Lord!

On the second day God made air . . .
On the third day God made land . . .
On the fourth day God made stars . . .
On the fifth day God made animals . . .
On the sixth day God made people . . .
On the seventh day God took a rest . . .

What things in Night-Light's basket did God create?

Giving God Thanks . . . a prayer to pray

Who made the flowers, the fields, and the trees? Who made the platypus, pine cones, and breeze? Why, our Lord God made all of these! And each time God created something new, he saw that it was good. Let's praise God for making the world so good and beautiful. After each line say, "God is good."

God made the flowers and the buzzy bees,
God is good.
God made the birds to nest in the trees.
God is good.
God made the mighty mountains tall,
God is good.
And fuzzy-wuzzy caterpillars sweet and small.
God is good.
God made the winds and the rains fly free.
God is good.
God made the world for you and ME!
God is good.

Here's a prayer for you to pray to thank our Creator for his loving way!

Dear God, we know you made the earth
And all the stars above—
You made the world then added us
So you'd have someone to love!
We love you, too, God! Amen.

God made the world and it was good, and all was new and bright—
Think of all God made for you as you drift to sleep. Night-night!

Point with me, one by one, and name all
the animals as Adam has done.

Names Are Nice

God said, "I have called you by name." Isaiah 43:1

Knowing God's Word . . . a story to read

Elephants, ostriches, kangaroos; wombats, wild cats, we love you! Which animal is your favorite? God gave Adam an important job. God told Adam to name the animals so we could tell them apart. Oh, what a job it was! So many animals, none looked the same; Adam gave each animal a very special name. I'm glad animals have names so we can tell them apart.

We have special names, too. My name is Night-Light. What's your name? When Mommy or Daddy calls your name, what do you do? You come! Did you know that God knows you and calls you by name, too? God loves us and calls us by name because he wants us to come to him. How do we know? The Bible tells us so!

GOD said, "I have called U by name."

Isaiah 43:1

Enjoying God's Gifts . . . a rhyme to say

Names are like special gifts we're given. Names tell who we are. Names help us know one another. And names are fun to say and learn! God has different names, too. Some people call God "Father." Some call him "Lord." But however we call on God's name, we know he loves us. God knows your name and loves you, too!

Here's a rhyme with lots of different names. As you listen, think about how glad you are for the gift of your name!

Aren't you glad that you have your name
Even though God loves us all the same?

For what if your name was Gippy McGee
Or Squiggle D. Do or U. Tickle Me?

Or Pick L. Jar or Tippy Toes?
Or Jiggly Jelly or Buttons N. Bows?

Your name is special and belongs to you
And helps others know you in all that you do.

So clap your hands and shout your name.
Aren't you glad God loves us all the same?

*Give each of Night-Light's
friends a special name.*

Giving God Thanks . . . a prayer to pray

Each animal has a special name so we can tell a mosquito from a moose and a guppy from a goose. But who gave you your special name? Maybe it was Mommy and Daddy or maybe you were named for your Grandma or Grandpa. Names help us know each other and tell each other apart. Let's praise God for our names. After each line, you can point upward and say, "We praise your name, Lord."

For kittens, canaries, and kangaroos,
We praise your name, Lord.
For Sallys, Sams, and Susie Q's,
We praise your name, Lord.
For whales, snails, and puppies with tails,
We praise your name, Lord.
For Jacks and Jills and Fionas and Phils,
We praise your name, Lord.
For every name, Lord, we thank you.
We praise your name, Lord.

Let's thank God for special names and for calling us his with a prayer.

Dear God, I'm glad I have a name
And that you know just who is who—
I'm happy that you know my name
And want me close to you. Amen.

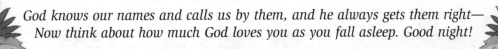

God knows our names and calls us by them, and he always gets them right—
Now think about how much God loves you as you fall asleep. Good night!

Who followed God's directions and built the ark?
Name everything you see that starts with the letter "A."

Always Obey

God said, "Obey me." Jeremiah 7:23

Knowing God's Word . . . a story to read

Let's play a game to see how well you follow directions! Clap your hands; tickle your toes; hop up and down; now wiggle your nose. Good for you! When we do what we're told to do, we obey. Do you remember Noah and his big, big boat? Noah loved God. And because Noah loved God, he obeyed God. When God told Noah to build a big boat, Noah obeyed. When God told Noah to let the animals into the ark, Noah obeyed. And when God told Noah to care for the animals, Noah obeyed. Noah always obeyed God and we can, too!

Obeying God and the people we love keeps us happy and safe. How do we know? The Bible tells us so!

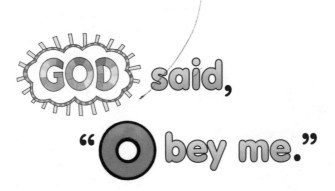

GOD said, "Obey me."

Jeremiah 7:23

Enjoying God's Gifts . . . a song to sing

When Daddy says, "Pick up your toys—you know how! It's time to get ready for bed now," what do you do? You obey him, of course! You obey Daddy because you love him. When we obey the people who love us, we show them our love. And when we obey God, we show God we love him, too! When we obey in all that we do, what a nice way to say, "I love you!" You can sing a fun song about obeying and saying, "I love you."

ALWAYS OBEY
(tune: *Three Blind Mice*)

Always obey! Always obey!
In all you do! And all you say!

Whenever we mind the way God wants us to,
And mind our Mommies and Daddies, too;

We'll bring smiles of love in all we do—
Always obey! Always obey!

How many clouds do you see? How many raindrops are falling?

Giving God Thanks . . . a prayer to pray

Did you know that all the world obeys God? When God said, "Let there be land," the earth obeyed. And when God told Noah to build the ark, Noah obeyed. Noah obeyed God because he loved God. We can obey God, too. Let's praise God for his great power and for all who obey him! You can tell how everyone obeyed God and make actions and sounds to go along.

God told Noah to build the ark—
And Noah obeyed God! Pound-pound!
   (make hammering motions)
God called the animals into the ark—
And the animals obeyed God! Growl-growl!
   (act like a lion)
God called the rains to tumble down—
And the rains obeyed God! Whoosh-whoosh!
   (make rain motions)
We praise God for the world and all that's in it,
And we want to obey God every minute!
   (give a high five)

Here's a prayer that we can pray to ask God's help so we'll always obey!

Dear God, you help us in every way
If we listen to you and choose to obey.
Please help us to do all the things you say.
And give us the strength to always obey.
We love you, God! Amen.

Obeying God means minding him and loving him with all our might—
Think of the ways you can obey God as you go to sleep. Night-night!

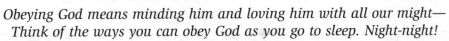

Point to and name all the colors in the rainbow.
Why did God put a rainbow in the sky for Noah?

Perfect Promises

God said, "What God promises, he keeps." Numbers 23:19

Knowing God's Word . . . a story to read

Here's a fun riddle for you. What does God give away yet always keep? His promises! God gives his promises to us and always keeps them, too. God promised Noah it would rain—and it rained. God promised Noah the rain would stop—and it stopped. And God promised Noah he'd be safe—and Noah was kept safe. Then God put a rainbow in the sky as a sign of his promise never to flood the world again. What a pretty way to remember God's promises!

Why does God make promises? Because he loves us! Why does God keep his promises? Because he loves us! And because God loves us, he keeps every promise he makes. How do we know? The Bible tells us so!

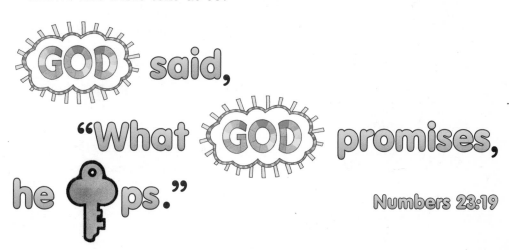

GOD said, "What GOD promises, he keeps."

Numbers 23:19

Enjoying God's Gifts . . . a rhyme to say

When Humpty Dumpty's shell broke, it couldn't be put back together again. That's how it is when we break our promises. Broken promises can't be put back together again. That's why unbroken promises are like special gifts! Unbroken promises are promises we can trust. God gives us promises we can always trust. And we can make promises others can trust. Repeat this fun rhyme and think about the gift of promises we can trust.

**Promises are like
Humpty Dumpty's shell—**
(sit on the floor or in bed)
**They'll crack and break
if we don't keep them well.**
(clap your hands)

**So whatever promise
you choose to make,**
(hold up one finger)
**Don't let your word fall
or your promise will break!**
(gently fall over)

**For promises broken,
no matter when,**
(hold up one finger)
Can't be put back together again.
(sadly shake your head)

*Which of these promises would you
rather have: one that's broken
or one that's unbroken?*

Giving God Thanks . . . a prayer to pray

Every day, all the time, God keeps his promises rain or shine! God has made many special promises. God promises to hear us. God promises to help us. God promises to love us. And what does God always do? God always keeps his promises! Let's praise God for his perfect promises. After each line clap and say, "God keeps his promises!"

God promises to stay here near us.
God keeps his promises!
God promises to always hear us.
God keeps his promises!
God promises to be forgiving.
God keeps his promises!
God promises his help in living.
God keeps his promises!
God promises his Word is true.
God keeps his promises!
God's promises are for me and you!
God keeps his promises!

Here's a prayer for you to pray to thank God for his promises every day!

Dear God, your love for us is so very deep
That the promises you make, you also keep.
We're thankful that we can trust in you
And in your perfect promises, too! Amen.

We can trust God's promises because he keeps them with all his might—
Now think of all God promises you as you drift to sleep. Good night!

*Find these story pictures: a banana, an orange rock,
the happy mouse, Night-Light, and a zebra.*

Love and Thanks

God said, "Show thanks to God." Psalm 50:14

Knowing God's Word . . . a story to read

What do you say when someone helps you? You say to that someone, "Thank you, thank you!" And what do you say if a gift comes to you? You say to the giver, "Thank you, thank you!" God helped Noah build the big ark to save the animals from the flood. God helped Noah care for the animals in the ark. God gave Noah the gift of love by keeping him safe. God helped Noah and gave him wonderful gifts. And guess what Noah said to God? Noah said, "Thank you, thank you!"

God helps us and gives us wonderful gifts, too! And what do we say to God? "Thank you, thank you!" God likes it when we say "thank you." How do we know? The Bible tells us so!

Psalm 50:14

Enjoying God's Gifts . . . a game to play

I love birthday parties, don't you? There are so many pretty packages to open and enjoy! Once, I found a new teddy bear in a gift! What gifts have you been given on your birthday? People give us gifts on our birthdays because they love us. It's the same with God's gifts, too. God helps us and gives us special gifts because he loves us! Just as God gave Noah the special gifts of his help and love, God gives us those wonderful gifts, too.

Let's give God a special gift. We can give the gift of thanks! When we give God a big "thank you," we show him our love.

Show God your love and thank him for the things on the flower petals. Now think: what else can you thank God for?

Giving God Thanks . . . a prayer to pray

God helps us every day in every way. And God gives us sweet gifts like love, sunshine, and rainbows! Let's praise and thank God for his sweet gifts. Point to each color in the rainbow. Then after each praise, you can say, "Thank you, God."

Red is for apples you made tasty and right,
Thank you, God.
Orange is for sunsets all fiery and bright.
Thank you, God.
Yellow's for buttercups, tiny but great,
Thank you, God.
Green is for peas that roll on my plate!
Thank you, God.
Blue is the sky, like an ocean of air,
Thank you, God.
Purple are flowers that bloom everywhere!
Thank you, God.
For the rainbow of things you give and you do,
We praise you, God, and say, "Thank you!"

Here's a prayer that you can pray to thank God for his love every day.

Dear God, you are so good to me!
You're as loving and kind as you can be.
From the evening stars to my morning toast,
You give me what my heart wants most.
Thank you and I love you! Amen.

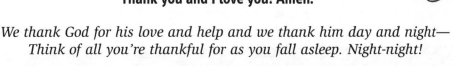

We thank God for his love and help and we thank him day and night—
Think of all you're thankful for as you fall asleep. Night-night!

Why did God tumble the tower of Babel?
How many red bricks do you see?

40

The One and Only

God said, "Remember that I am God." Isaiah 46:9

Knowing God's Word . . . a story to read

Do you remember the Tower of Babel and the people who built it so high? The people thought they could be as wise as God if their tower touched the sky. But only God is wisest of all, so he tumbled that tower—oh my!

The people who built the Tower of Babel thought they were smart. But they were oh so wrong! If they had learned God's Word, they would have learned that only God is wiser than anyone. They would have learned that only God is more powerful than anyone. And they would have learned that we are to honor and praise only God! How do we know? The Bible tells us so!

GOD said, "Remember that am GOD."

Isaiah 46:9

Enjoying God's Gifts . . . a game to play

I like gifts, don't you? If you could have any gift in the world, what would you choose? A new ball and bat, a pony, or cat? How 'bout a bike with shiny red wheels or ice cream for every one of your meals? A king in the Bible chose the gift of being wise. King Solomon asked God to help him learn many things. So God gave Solomon the gift of wisdom. And God gives us the gift of wisdom, too. When we want to learn about God, he helps us. God helps us learn his Word. God helps us learn ways to praise him. And God helps us pray, too.

Pretend to unwrap your special gift from God. Now put on your thinking cap and let's see what you've learned!

Who is wiser than anyone? *God!*

Who controls the stars and sun? *God!*

Who hears our prayers each day and night? *God!*

Who do we love with all our might? *God!*

Who will help us make wise choices?

Giving God Thanks . . . a prayer to pray

God wants us to know there is no one wiser or stronger than he is. Let's praise God using our hands in a fun way.

Not just a bit of praise—
(hands on the floor)
Not just a little praise.
(hands at knees)
Not just small praise—
(hands at shoulders)
Give God TALL praise!
(hands high in the air)

Praise that reaches way up high—
(point upward)
Praise so tall it taps the sky!
(jump and point upward)
We praise God because he's wise—
(tap your head)
Lift your hands, let your praises rise!
(stretch hands in the air)

Let's honor God with a prayer to thank him for being smarter and stronger than anyone.

Dear God, you are the only one
Who rules the night and commands the sun.
Please help us know, please open our eyes,
To see that no one but you is as strong or wise! Amen.

God is wiser than anyone and is stronger in his might—
Now think about all he teaches you as you go to sleep. Night, night!

Point to the items Abraham may have taken on his trip.
What items would you take on a trip?

Just Trust!

God said, "They will trust in the Lord." Zephaniah 3:12

Knowing God's Word . . . a story to read

Have you ever moved to a new home? It can be fun to move, but it can be a little scary, too. Will I like my new home or the friends I meet there? Will I still have my bed and my favorite chair? That's what Abraham felt when God told him to move to a new home. Abraham wasn't sure about moving, so he prayed and asked God's help. Then Abraham trusted God and followed him. Abraham knew God would take care of him in his new home. And guess what? God did! Abraham trusted and believed in God's care, and liked his new home when he finally got there! We can trust God, too. How do we know? The Bible tells us so!

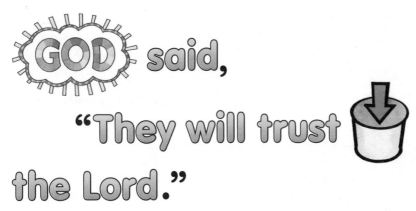

GOD said, "They will trust the Lord."

Zephaniah 3:12

Enjoying God's Gifts . . . a song to sing

I like trusting God, don't you? When I trust God to be with me, I know that he is there. And when I trust God to hear me, he hears my every prayer. If I trust God to help me, he stays right by my side. And when I trust God to love me, I feel all warm inside. Can you find the gift with the word "trust" on it? Trusting God is like a special gift from God to us. And the gift of trust makes me feel so good I could sing! Let's sing a song about trusting God. You can point to the letters in the word "trust" as we sing.

What gift did God give Abraham that he also gives you?

TRUST
(tune: *Bingo*)

**We always know
what God will do**

**Because he tells us
and it's true—**

**T-R-U-S-T
T-R-U-S-T
T-R-U-S-T**

Have trust, you really must!

Giving God Thanks . . . a prayer to pray

Can you say "trust?" It's a small word but means big things! Trusting God means we know he will do what he promises. (And God always keeps his promises!) Trusting God means knowing he will love us. Trusting God means knowing he will help us. And trusting God shows him our love, too. Now say, "Trust, trust, we really must." We really must trust God every day and night, and God will help us through his power and might! Let's praise God for the trust he helps us have. After each line shout, "Trust, trust, we really must!"

For God's help in all we do,
Trust, trust, we really must!
For God's love toward me and you,
Trust, trust, we really must!
For every time God hears a prayer,
Trust, trust, we really must!
We praise you, God, for being there!
Trust, trust, we really must!

Let's offer God a thank-you prayer for helping us trust him and being there!

Dear God, it feels so good to trust in you
'Cuz we know you'll help us in all we do.
Please help us have trust in a really big way
So we can follow you closer every day! Amen.

God helps us trust him every day and during every night—
Now think of ways you trust God as you go to sleep. Good night!

Point to baby Isaac. Find all the other "B" words:
bell, books, blanket, bunny, basket, ball, and bowl.

Promise of Love

God said, "What God promises, he keeps." Numbers 23:19

Knowing God's Word . . . a story to read

What do you say when you clasp hands to pray? Do you tell God you love him with the words that you say or thank God for the blessings he brings every day? Praying is a good way to talk to God, but will he hear us? Oh yes! God promises to hear our prayers and answer them, too.

Abraham and Sarah prayed. They prayed and asked God for a baby to love. And what did God do? God promised Abraham and Sarah a baby to love. Did God keep his promise? Oh yes! God sent them a baby to love and to hold; a baby to cuddle as they grew old! God promises to hear and answer our prayers. And we know that God always keeps his promises! How do we know? The Bible tells us so!

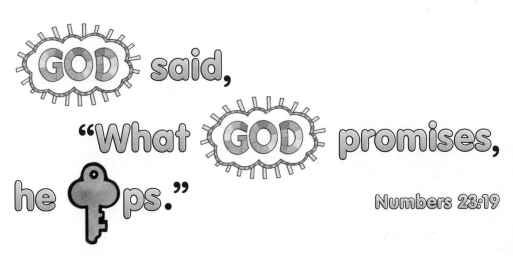

GOD said, "What GOD promises, he keeps."

Numbers 23:19

Enjoying God's Gifts . . . a rhyme to say

What's the best gift you ever had? Was it a fluffy bear or a shiny new bike or striped underwear? Gifts are happy things, aren't they? Abraham and Sarah's favorite gift was the gift of their baby Isaac. They were so happy with their new baby, they laughed and giggled with joy! They named the baby Isaac which means "laughter." What a giggly, wiggly, bundle of joy was the perfect gift of their baby boy!

God's promises are like special gifts to us, too. God promises to be near us, to help us, to forgive us, and to love us. Aren't those wonderful gifts? Let's say a fun rhyme to remind us of God's perfect promises for you and me and how he keeps them perfectly!

What colors are in baby bear's blanket?

Pat-a-cake, pat-a-cake,
what do you see?

God's perfect promises
for you and me!

Roll 'em,
and pat 'em,
and mark 'em with a P,

God's perfect promises
for you and me!

Giving God Thanks . . . a prayer to pray

God promised Abraham many things. God promised to help Abraham move to a new home—and he did! God promised to stay with Abraham all the time—and he did! God promised Abraham he and Sarah would have a baby. And they did! What do you say when someone does something wonderful for you? You say, "thank you." And that's just what Abraham and Sarah said to God. We can praise and thank God for keeping his promises, too. After each line, say, "We thank you, Lord."

For promising to hear us,
  We thank you, Lord.
For promising to stay near us,
  We thank you, Lord.
For promising us your loving care,
  We thank you, Lord.
For promising to help and always be there,
  We thank you, Lord.

Let's share a prayer and thank God that he hears us and promises to always stay near us.

Dear God, we thank you for hearing each prayer
And for your promise to always be there.
Your promises are perfect, powerful, and true
And for keeping your promises, we're
      thankful to you! Amen.

God gives us his promises to hold onto tight—
Think of all God promises as you go to sleep. Night-night!

Who protected baby Moses?
How many flowers and butterflies do you see by the river?

Safe and Sound

God said, "I will save you." Jeremiah 30:10

Knowing God's Word . . . a story to read

Cuddle in your blankets, now cuddle down. Don't you feel all safe and sound? Being held or cuddled is nice, isn't it? It makes us feel warm and loved and very safe. That's how baby Moses felt when his mommy put him in a snug basket. Moses' mommy knew that God would keep her baby safe and sound, cuddled and warm; that God would protect her baby and keep him from harm.

Smiling in his basket boat, bobbing up and down—
God watched baby Moses and kept him safe and sound.

God protected baby Moses and God promises to watch over us and keep us safe, too. How do we know? The Bible tells us so!

Jeremiah 30:10

Enjoying God's Gifts . . . a rhyme to say

Gifts are fun, aren't they? The very best gifts are made with lots of love. All of God's gifts are made with love. Why does God give us the gift of being safe each day and night? It's because God loves us very much and holds us close and tight! God's gift of being safe and sound shows that God loves us. Now that's a fine gift, isn't it? Can you answer these questions about being safe?

- *How did God keep baby Moses safe?*
- *How do you keep your milk safe from spilling?*
- *How does God keep you safe?*

**Safe and sound,
safe and sound—**

**God is watching
all around.**

**God keeps us safe
both night and day**

**So we're safe and sound
in every way!**

What happened to Moses after God kept him safe? God will keep you safe because he loves you, too!

Giving God Thanks . . . a prayer to pray

How do you keep your milk safe and sound with no spills? You watch over your cup! You watch over your cup and try not to tip it as you enjoy your milk and happily sip it. God keeps us safe by watching over us, too. Who is with us all the time? God is with us all the time. God is with us and watches over us. And God keeps us safe.

Let's praise and thank God for keeping us safe with a fun rhyme. Put on your pretend binoculars and look at all the things God sees.

**God watches over the good night moon,
God watches over my little room.
God watches over my cozy bed
And the puffy pillow where I lay my head.
God watches over my favorite toys
And knows what makes each nighttime noise.
God watches over me all through the night,
So I am safe and sleep so tight.**

Let's ask God to watch over us all day and night.

**Dear God, we pray and ask of you
To keep us safe in all we do.
Stay above us,
Always love us;
Thank you, God, we love you. Amen.**

*God is watching over us and keeps us safe as he holds us tight—
Now think of ways God keeps you safe as you fall asleep. Good night!*

What did God say to Moses from the burning bush?
How are the birds being helpers?

God's Special Helper

God said, "You may serve me." Jeremiah 15:19

Knowing God's Word . . . a story to read

Clean your room, pick up your toys, when Daddy is sleeping, shhh, no noise! Toss away your napkin when you are done, isn't being a helper lots of fun? Moses was a special helper, too. Moses was God's special helper. God had an important job for Moses to do. What do you think Moses said when God asked him to help? Moses said, "I'll be God's helper—special and true and do all the things God tells me to do!"

Moses was God's special helper—that's true; he did everything God asked him to do. But why? Moses served God because he loved God. Moses helped God with a willing heart. And God was happy. That's because God wants us to be his special helpers. How do we know? The Bible tells us so!

GOD said, "U may serve me."

Jeremiah 15:19

Enjoying God's Gifts . . . a rhyme to say

When we serve and help God, we give him the gift of our love. And we all like gifts, right? It's fun to be God's special helper. And it's nice to give God special gifts, too! There are so many ways we can be good helpers. Why, you can even help Mommy or Daddy put you to bed. Here's a bedtime-helper rhyme so you can help at beddy time!

**I can smooth the blankets
on my comfy cozy bed;**

**I can fluff the pillow
where I lay my sleepy head.**

**I can pull my blankets up
around my chin like this;**

**But now I need some special help
with a loving good-night kiss!**

*How is Night-Light being a helper?
How many dishes do you see?*

Giving God Thanks . . . a prayer to pray

I like being a helper! I help around the house in different ways. I always put away my toys and feed my little fishes; I wash my teddy's jacket, and I dry the dinner dishes.

There are many ways to serve God. Let's praise God for helping us serve him in wonderful ways! You can help by saying, "I'm God's special helper" at the right time.

I tell others about God and his love.
I'm God's special helper.
I say my prayers to God above.
I'm God's special helper.
I learn God's Word that's always true.
I'm God's special helper.
I help serve God by helping you.
I'm God's special helper.
I praise you, God for helping me
Be the best helper I can be!
I'm God's special helper.

Let's share a prayer and ask God to make us his good helpers.

Dear God, I want to be your helper
In all I say and all I do.
Please stay beside me and always guide me
As I work to help and serve you. Amen.

We can be God's helpers and serve him with a smile that's bright—
Now think of ways to be God's helper as you fall asleep. Good night!

Find Moses' staff. How did God use Moses' staff to keep his people safe? Count the fish in the sea.

Safe in God's Love

God said, "I will save you." Jeremiah 30:10

Knowing God's Word . . . a story to read

1, 2, 3, 4, 5— *(count on your fingers)*
I caught a little fish alive *(make "swimmy" hands)*
And held him safe and sound. *(cup your hands)*
6, 7, 8, 9, 10— *(count on your fingers)*
Then I let him go again *(make "swimmy" hands)*
In his fishy pond. *(cup your hands)*

That was fun, wasn't it? You held the fishy safe in your hands, then you let him go again. Did you know that God holds us safe and sound, too? Moses ran from a mean king and came to the big, deep sea. How could Moses get across as safe as safe can be? God helped Moses! God parted that sea and kept Moses safe as he could be. And God saves and guides us, too. How do we know? The Bible tells us so!

GOD said, "I will save U."

Jeremiah 30:10

Enjoying God's Gifts . . . a song to sing

How does it feel to be safe as can be? It's like a wonderful warm hug inside of me! It feels so nice to know that I can trust God like Moses did. I can trust God to guard me and guide me and stay right beside me. Trusting God and feeling safe are two wonderful gifts God gives us. We can give God a special gift, too. Let's sing a fun song to thank God for loving us and saving us.

SAFE & SOUND
(tune: Row Your Boat)

Run, run, Moses run
(run in place)
As fast as you can flee—
God will keep you safe and sound
Just as he does for me!

Walk, walk, Moses walk
(walk in place)
Across the parted sea—
God will keep you safe and sound
Just as he does for me!

Smile, smile, Moses smile
(smile and point upward)
Safe as safe can be—
God has kept you safe from harm
Just as he does for me!

Find the shadows.
Name the shapes.

Giving God Thanks . . . a prayer to pray

Moses ran to the sea and stood beside it, and God kept him safe when he chose to divide it. God parted the sea so Moses could be safe and free. And what did Moses do then? Moses thanked God and praised him, too." Let's praise God for keeping us safe by saying, "God saves us!" at the right time.

Who saves us through his power?
God saves us!
Who saves us through his might?
God saves us!
Who keeps us safe within his love all the day and night?
God saves us!
Who can we trust to help us?
God saves us!
Who will always guide us?
God saves us!
Who keeps us safe within his love and always stays beside us?
God saves us!

Now we can thank God with a prayer for keeping us safe and sound.

Dear God, we pray and ask of you
To hold us safe in all we do.
Stay above us,
Always love us;
Thank you, God, we love you. Amen.

God keeps us safe and guides us with his loving power and might—
Think about how safe you feel as you fall asleep. Good night!

What did God do when his people asked for food?
Find the striped bird eating its dinner.

God Will Answer

God said, "I will answer you." Jeremiah 33:3

Knowing God's Word . . . a story to read

Grrrowl! Can you hear my tummy growling as you sit over there? I'm so very hungry, I think I could eat a bear! What do you do when you're hungry? You ask for something to eat or munch. Then Daddy answers and brings you something for lunch. God's people were as hungry as could be after they walked across the wide Red Sea. Their tummies mumbled and the people grumbled, "We want something to eat!" Moses asked God for food and what do you think God did? God heard the people and answered them. God sent them sweet manna to munch and the people were happy after their yummy lunch.

God hears each word we say and every "amen" when we pray. But the best part is oh so true, God promises to answer, too! How do we know? The Bible tells us so!

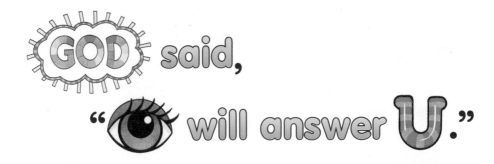

GOD said, "I will answer U."

Jeremiah 33:3

65

Enjoying God's Gifts . . . a game to play

Once I was very hungry for a cookie. Guess what I had to eat instead? I had spinach! Mommy answered when I was hungry, but she answered in her own way. I guess spinach is better for me when I'm feeling munchy—but I wish Mommy had answered differently. God hears what we ask him and God will answer. But God answers in his own way. God knows what's best for us and his answers are always good and right. I'm so glad God hears each word I say and answers in his time and way!

Let's play a hearing and answering game. Listen carefully for the question, then you can answer in your own way.

 Who hears every word we say?
God hears.

 Who answers in his time and way?
God answers.

 How did God answer his people when their tummies grumbled?
God gave them food.

 Why did God hear his people when they mumbled?
Because God loved his people.

Night-Light is praying. What might he be saying?

66

Giving God Thanks . . . a prayer to pray

God hears us when we shout or call, he hears us when we whisper small; God knows our needs before we do; God hears and he will answer, too. Isn't it wonderful to know God hears us all the time and answers in his time and way? Let's praise God together for the wonderful way God hears and answers us. After each line, clap two times and say, "God will answer me!"

What if you ask God for a happy day?
God will answer me!
What if you ask God's help to pray?
God will answer me!
What if you ask to be kind and sweet?
God will answer me!
What if you ask for good food to eat?
God will answer me!
We can ask God for whatever we need
And know God will answer in his own way and speed.
God will answer me!

Let's share a prayer that God will hear,
'cuz prayers are sweet to our Father's ear!

Dear God, we're glad you lend your ear
And take the time to really hear.
You promise to hear us because you stay near us
And answer our prayers every day of the year.
I love you, God! Amen.

God hears and answers us through his loving power and might—
Think of how God hears you say, "I love you" every night. Sleep tight!

How many stone tablets did God use for his rules?

Rules Rule!

God said, "Obey me." Jeremiah 7:23

Knowing God's Word . . . a story to read

There are rules at home and rules at school. There are rules at church and at the playground. Why are there rules we have to obey? To keep us happy and safe at work or play! God gave us the most important rules to obey. God gave us ten important rules called the Ten Commandments. Can you count to ten? 1-2-3-4-5-6-7-8-9-10. Ten rules God gave us to always obey; ten rules to follow in every way.

What do you do when Daddy says to put your toys away? You pick up your toys and quickly obey. We can obey God by praying and thanking him and learning his Word. God wants us to choose to obey him! How do we know? The Bible tells us so!

Enjoying God's Gifts . . . a song to sing

Go! Stop! Shhh—don't talk!
Stop! Go! Wait—don't walk!
Enter, exit, only one way—
Rules are made for us to obey!

Whenever we do what we're told to do, we obey. Obeying shows others we respect them. And obeying God's ten special rules shows God we love him, too. God gave us his rules as special gifts to keep us safe and happy. We can give God the gift of love by obeying his rules. When we obey God in all that we do, what a nice way to say, "I love you!" Let's sing a fun song to God about obeying and saying, "I love you." You can march and clap in time to the tune.

ALWAYS OBEY
(tune: *Three Blind Mice*)

Always obey! Always obey!
In all you do! And all you say!

Whenever we mind the way God wants us to,
And mind our Mommies and Daddies, too;

We'll bring smiles of love in all we do—
Always obey! Always obey!

Find Night-Light's signs: Stop,
Go, Don't Walk, One Way.
What does each sign mean?

Giving God Thanks . . . a prayer to pray

What rules do you have in your home? Rules are made to keep us safe and happy. Rules are made to be obeyed. God's Ten Commandments keep us safe and happy when we obey them. But what are God's ten special rules? Let's find out as we praise God for keeping us safe and happy. Hold up the right number of fingers every time you hear a number word.

Ten rules God gave us to always obey;
Ten rules to follow in every way.
Rule 1—God is our only God.
Rule 2—Worship God, the only one.
Rule 3—Always love and respect God's name.
Rule 4—Take a rest from all your fun.
Rule 5—Love your mommy and daddy.
Rule 6—Never hurt anyone.
Rule 7—Husbands and wives be true to each other.
Rule 8—Never steal from anyone.
Rule 9—Please don't ever tell a lie.
Rule 10—Be happy with what you own.

Let's thank God for his ten special rules with a special prayer.

Dear God, thank you for the ten special rules
You gave us to always obey—
Please help us follow each important rule
As well as we can each day. Amen.

God gave us his rules to follow each day and every night—
Think of how God's rules keep you safe as you go to sleep. Sleep tight!

How did God help Joshua?
Count the orange stones in the wall.

A Tower of Help and Power

God said, "I will help you." Isaiah 41:10

Knowing God's Word . . . a story to read

Try to lift the corner of your bed. Ugh! It's too heavy for only one, you need help to get the job done! Ask Mommy or Daddy to help you and you will see that a helping hand is what you need. There are many times we need help and God is always ready and willing to help us in mighty ways. Joshua had a big job to do. Joshua and God's soldiers needed to get over the walls of Jericho. But me-oh-my, those walls were tall—how could the soldiers get over them all? With God's help, that's how! Joshua asked God to help him. Then Joshua followed God's directions. Joshua and God's soldiers marched around, and with God's help the walls fell down—ta-daa!

We can count on God when we ask him for help. How do we know? The Bible tells us so!

GOD said, "👁 will help U."

Isaiah 41:10

Enjoying God's Gifts . . . a rhyme to say

Think of all the ways God helped Joshua and the soldiers. God helped by hearing their prayers. God helped by answering them. God helped by telling Joshua how to march around the walls. And God helped with his mighty power to tumble those giant walls. Ta-daa! Isn't God's help great? When we need help throughout our days, God gives us help in many ways. How does God help us? Let's find out!

God helps us grow up straight and tall, *(stand up tall)*
And helps by answering when we call; *(shout, "I love you, God!")*
God helps us when we're feeling bad, *(look sad)*
And turns our hearts from sad to glad. *(smile)*
God helps us say our prayers at night, *(fold hands in prayer)*
And helps us sleep so sweet and tight! *(pretend to sleep)*

Point to the face that shows how you feel.
No matter how you feel today, God will help you in every way.

Giving God Thanks . . . a prayer to pray

Can you count to seven with me? 1-2-3-4-5-6-7. Good for you! Think of all the sevens in the story of Joshua and the giant walls of Jericho. There were seven priests with seven horns and God's soldiers marched for seven morns. Around they marched seven times in all and when the horns tooted, down came the walls! The number seven reminds us of God and of his help. Why, before we can count to seven, God sends us mighty help from heaven! We can have fun counting to seven and remembering God's powerful help.

1-2-3-4-5-6-7—7 priests followed Joshua.
(march in place)
1-2-3-4-5-6-7—7 horns they blew, TA-DAA!
(blow pretend horns)
1-2-3-4-5-6-7—7 times they marched around;
(march in place)
Then through God's power the walls fell down! TA-DAA!
(blow pretend horns)

Now here's a prayer for us to say to thank God for his powerful help each day.

Dear God, you're more powerful than anyone
And through your help we can get the job done.
We give you thanks for the help and love
You send our way from Heaven above.
We love you, Lord! Amen.

God helps us in so many ways through his perfect power and might—
Think of all God's loving help as you go to sleep. Night-night!

What is Night-Light sharing with his friends? Who was Naomi's friend?

Fine Friends

God said, "Love your neighbor." Leviticus 19:18

Knowing God's Word . . . a story to read

Who loves to stop and play awhile? Who always leaves you with a smile? Who is so friendly? Why, your friends, of course! Ruth and Naomi were best friends. They helped and shared with one another and showed God's love to each other. Naomi told Ruth all about God and Ruth shared her food with Naomi. What good friends they were!

Think of all the friends you have: friends you meet at the swimming pool, friends in church, friends at school. Your family is full of friendly friends—just think of all the love God sends! And God wants us to love our friends and neighbors and show them his love, too. How do we know? The Bible tells us so!

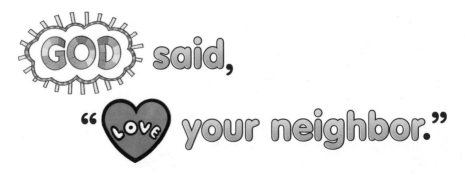

GOD said, "LOVE your neighbor."

Leviticus 19:18

Enjoying God's Gifts . . . a song to sing

Why were Ruth and Naomi such good friends? They were good friends because they loved God and they cared for each other. Ruth and Naomi knew that good friends are gifts from God. Our friends are gifts from God, too. Friends are gifts God gives us from above, and the best way to thank God is to show friends our love! I like doing nice things for my friends and showing them my love. It makes me feel so cozy and happy inside. Let's sing a happy song for God and our friends. Then we can show them we're happy we know them!

THE KINDNESS SONG
(tune: *Ten Little Indians*)

**Be kind and loving to one another,
Be forgiving of each other—**

**Show your love in all you do
'Cuz that's how God loves you!**

How many friends are with Night-Light?

Giving God Thanks . . . a prayer to pray

Cut out two paper hearts. Hold your paper hearts and tell the names of two friends you play with, two friends from school or church, and two friends in your family. I'm happy there are so many friends to be thankful for, aren't you? Let's praise and thank God for friends to care for and friends to love, for all the

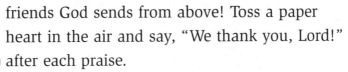

friends God sends from above! Toss a paper heart in the air and say, "We thank you, Lord!" after each praise.

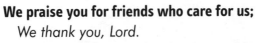

We praise you for friends who care for us;
We thank you, Lord.
We praise you for friends who share with us.
We thank you, Lord.
We praise you for every person you send;
We thank you, Lord.
We praise you for being our best friend!
We thank you, Lord.

Here's a prayer for us to say to thank God for sending friends our way.

Dear God, we're glad you send to us
Friends who love and care for us.
Please help us be kind to every friend
Whom you take the time to send. Amen.

God sends friends for us to love and who make our hearts feel light—
Think of all the friends you have as you go to sleep. Good night!

What did Samuel hear God say? Find five stars,
a yellow moon, a mouse, and Night-Light's teddy bear.

Listen Up!

God said, "Listen to me." Isaiah 51:1

Knowing God's Word . . . a story to read

Close your eyes and listen. What do you hear? Maybe you hear a parakeet singing or the furnace chugging or a bell ringing. There are so many wonderful sounds in our world! Samuel knew there were wonderful sounds, too. But he heard the most glorious sound there ever could be! It wasn't a drum or bugle or horn; it wasn't a lark that heralds the morn. What Samuel heard was much sweeter. Samuel heard God's voice calling his name! Three times God called Samuel's name. What do you think Samuel said to God? Samuel told God he was listening—and that's the best thing to do when God calls!

God likes it when we listen to him, too. How do we know? The Bible tells us so!

GOD said, "Listen 2 me."

Isaiah 51:1

Enjoying God's Gifts . . . a game to play

Cover the letters H and T. What does e-a-r spell? It spells the word "ear." When we listen, we usually listen with our ears. But there is another way we can listen to God. Uncover the letters H and the letter T. What does h-e-a-r-t spell? It spells the word "heart!" We can listen to God with our hearts by the feelings he gives us. Now cover the letter T. Point to the letters h-e-a-r. They spell the word "hear." What a special gift it is to hear God in so many ways! Let's give God a special gift with a rhyme about hearing. Cover and uncover the letters in the word "heart" to help.

We lend an ear
(cover the H and T)
To listen and hear
(cover just the T)
That is how it starts;
But when we choose to hear our God,
(cover the T)
We listen with our hearts!
(uncover the whole word)

Giving God Thanks . . . a prayer to pray

Whisper something in my ear and I will tell you what I hear. What did you whisper? What did I hear? We speak in many ways. We speak in whispers and in the way we touch each other, too. What do hugs say? They say, "I love you!" God speaks to us in different ways, too. God speaks to us through his words in the Bible, through other people, and by the feelings he gives our hearts. Let's praise God for what he says to me and you, and the ways he tells us, "I love you." You can cup your ear and say, "We thank you, God" after each praise.

For people who bring an encouraging word,
We thank you, God.
For wonderful words in the Bible we've heard,
We thank you, God.
For helping our hearts hear all that you say,
We thank you, God.
We praise and thank you every day!
We thank you, God.

Now here's a prayer that we can pray to ask God's help in listening each day.

Dear God, please help us always listen to you
And follow your desires in all that we do.
For the sweetest sounds that will ever be heard
Are your voice of truth and your holy Word! Amen.

God speaks to us in many ways and we can listen with all our might—
Think of the ways God speaks his love as you fall asleep. Night-night!

What was David doing when God chose him to be king?
How many sheep is David watching in Night-Light's picture?

God's Choice

God said, "The Lord looks at the heart." 1 Samuel 16:7

Knowing God's Word . . . a story to read

Hold up your blanket and pillow. If you could choose to sleep with one, which would you choose? Would it be the blanket because it's blue, or the pillow that you'd use? We often choose because of looks, of color and of size. But when God makes a choice, he sees through different eyes. Remember when God chose David to be king? God could have chosen the tallest or oldest man. But instead, God chose young David.

God sees our outsides, but that's just a part—when God looks at us, he looks at our hearts! Are you kind to others and love God a lot? Do you use all the kindness and caring you've got? That's what God looks at! How do we know? The Bible tells us so!

GOD said, "The Lord looks at the ♥."

1 Samuel 16:7

Enjoying God's Gifts . . . a song to sing

Are you big or small or short or tall? Do you have curly hair that stays in place or lots of freckles on your face? No matter how you look, God loves you! Isn't that wonderful? God cares more about what nice things are in your heart. God saw the kindness and strength in David and chose David to be king. God chooses you for his plans, too. And God chooses you by looking at your heart. What a gift of love it is when God chooses you to serve him! Let's celebrate this gift of love with a song to God!

CHOOSE ME, LORD
(tune: *Silent Night*)

Choose me, Lord—use me, Lord.
What I want to do is serve you.

I'm so glad that you see the part
Of lovingkindness inside my heart.

Choose me, Lord, choose me—
Use me, Lord, use me.

*Find David (he's the smallest brother). Find these brothers:
the curly haired, the tallest, and the oldest brother.*

Giving God Thanks . . . a prayer to pray

Would you rather choose spinach or carrots for lunch? Would you rather have bananas or grapes by the bunch? Would you rather have pets of goldfish or mice? Would you rather treat somebody naughty or nice? We have lots of choices to make each day and we want to choose carefully. That's how God chose David to be king. God chose wisely because he knew David was loving and strong. God chose David to serve him and God chooses us to serve him, too. Let's praise God for choosing us. You can choose the praise you'll use!

**Clap your hands or stomp your feet—
the way God sees us can't be beat!
Give a hop or smile wide—
God can see our hearts inside!
Nod your head or give a bow—
God chooses us to serve him now.
Tap your toes or shout, "I love you!"—
God wants us to choose him, too!**

Let's thank God for looking at us in such a special way.

**Dear God, I'm so very glad you see
The loving heart inside of me.
I'm glad you see my feelings, too
And know how much I love you! Amen.**

*God looks inside our hearts and oh, what a beautiful sight!
Think of how God sees you as you go to sleep. Good night!*

How many stones did David have for his sling? How many stones did David need to bring down Goliath with God's help?

Giant Strength

God said, "I will make you strong." Isaiah 45:5

Knowing God's Word . . . a story to read

Can you tap your head, then tickle your toes? Can you turn around and touch your nose? Can you bend your arm and kiss your elbow? Of course not! There are some things that seem impossible to do. It seemed impossible for small David to fight giant Goliath. But even though David was small, his love for God was oh-so-tall! David asked God to make him strong, and what happened then? David swung his sling 'round and 'round, and—zing! plop!—Goliath fell down!

If you're afraid of thunder, who helps you be strong? And when you're feeling not-so-brave, who helps you get along? You may have lots of people who love and help you, but no one is as big or strong as God is! God will always help you be strong when you ask him. How do we know? The Bible tells us so!

GOD said, "👁 will make U strong."

Isaiah 45:5

Enjoying God's Gifts . . . a game to play

How tall are you? Have Mommy or Daddy measure you with a long piece of thread or string. Now hold your string against the wall and look upward. The ceiling is way up high, isn't it? Mean old Goliath was even taller than the ceiling! Now that's tall! But was Goliath bigger than God? Oh, no! God is bigger than anyone or anything. And God is stronger than anyone, too. Isn't it wonderful to know that our bigger-than-anything God helps us and makes us strong? What a gift it is to have God's loving help and strength. Why, it makes me feel like marching with joy! Here are words for you to shout and let your joy for God come out!

BIGGER THAN ANYTHING!

Let us shout!
Let us sing!
God is bigger than anything!
We can go to any length
With God's power and his strength!

Night-Light has a big job to do! Who can help him? Help Night-Light find all the triangles.

Giving God Thanks . . . a prayer to pray

David wasn't very big; he was really sort of small—but when he asked for God to help, his strength grew really tall! David learned that God makes us strong and brave. And David learned that God is bigger than anyone or anything. Let's praise God with a fun action rhyme. Follow along with the actions and words as you praise and thank God for making us strong.

Can you clap your hands today?
I can do it right away!
(clap hands)

I can go to any length
When I ask God for help and strength!

(Repeat using the following questions and actions.)
- **Can you stomp your feet today?**
- **Can you twirl around today?**
- **Can you touch your toes today?**

Here's a prayer that we can pray to ask God for strength every day.

Dear God, we ask you for strength
To live for you each day.
Please help us grow so strong and brave
In all we do and say.
We love you! Amen.

God is bigger than anything and we are strong in his might—
Just think of how God makes you brave as you go to sleep. Night-night!

In what way is Night-Light thanking God?
How did David thank God? Find the frog.

Thank You, God!

God said, "Show thanks to God." Psalm 50:14

Knowing God's Word . . . a story to read

What are three of the nicest words that anyone can say? They are "Please" and "Thank you" and should be said all through the day. When we ask for something, what do we say? We say, "Please." And when we receive something, what do we say? We say, "Thank you." We ask God for many things and he gives us such wonderful gifts. What do we want to say to God? We want to say, "Thank you!" David wanted to thank God for his blessings, too. He thanked God with prayers and with songs on the harp— plink-plink! And David thanked God with beautiful poems.

When we learn God's Word and speak it, we are telling God we love him. What a wonderful thank-you that is! How do we know? The Bible tells us so!

GOD said, "Show thanks 2 GOD."

Psalm 50:14

Enjoying God's Gifts . . . a song to sing

What do you say when you receive special gifts? You say ahs and oos and oh-thank-yous! Special gifts need special thank-yous. God gives us the most special gifts of all. God's gifts are called blessings and God blesses us each day with help and love sent from above. Special blessings need special thank-yous, too. When we live with a thankful heart every day, we're like a wonderful, living thank-you card to God! Let's give God a special thank you with a song.

THANK YOU, THANK YOU, LORD ABOVE
(tune: *Twinkle, Twinkle Little Star*)

Thank you, thank you, Lord above,
For your blessings sent with love.
I want to live my life anew
As a thank-you card for you—
Thank you, thank you, Lord above,
For your blessings sent with love.

Which of these hearts matches the hearts on the table?

Giving God Thanks . . . a prayer to pray

What are ways you say "thank you" to someone? You can send a pretty card that gives the heart a tug; you might want to sing a song or give a kiss and hug. There are lots of ways to say "thank you" to God, too. Have Mommy or Daddy help you write "Thank you, God" on one side of a card and "I love you!" on the other side. Can you read the words? Let's use your thank-you card to give God special praise and thanks. After each line, hold up your card and say, "Thank you, God. I love you!"

For all the loving things you do,
Thank you, God. I love you.
For blessing us each day anew,
Thank you, God. I love you!
For taking the time to teach us, too,
Thank you, God. I love you!
We want to praise and say, "Thank you!"
Thank you, God. I love you!

Another way we can thank God is with a special prayer!

Dear God, you are so loving
And give us gifts each day.
You show your loving care for us
In every word and way.
Thank you, God, for loving me! Amen.

Thank God for his perfect love and blessings bright—
Think of ways to thank him as you fall asleep. Good night!

How many coins do you see? What did God give to Solomon?

Wise and Wonderful

God said, "I will give you wisdom." 1 Kings 3:12

Knowing God's Word . . . a story to read

If you could have anything you asked for, what would you want? Maybe you'd like ice cream for your meals or a shiny red bike with silvery wheels. God told King Solomon he could have anything he wanted. What did King Solomon ask for? He asked God for wisdom to help him be a good king. Now, that was a wise thing to ask for! God was so pleased with Solomon, he gave the king lots of gold and sparkly jewels!

Where does being wise come from? Does it come from swimming pools or lots of gold and sparkly jewels? Does wisdom come from heavy books or is it found in people's looks? No! All wisdom comes from God. How do we know? The Bible tells us so!

GOD said, " will give U wisdom."

1 Kings 3:12

Enjoying God's Gifts . . . a game to play

King Solomon could have had anything he wanted. He could have chosen gold and jewels or mansions built with swimming pools. But instead, Solomon chose to ask God to make him smart and kind. And what did God do? God gave Solomon the gift of wisdom. Being wise helped Solomon be a good and kind king. With God's wisdom, Solomon knew how to lead his people and bring them closer to God. What a wise king Solomon was! Let's see how wise you are. Can you answer these story questions? Touch a question mark each time you answer a question.

Who asked God to help him be wise and kind?
King Solomon

Where does wisdom come from?
God

Why is it good to ask God for wisdom?
So we can make good choices.

How can the Bible help us be wise?
The Bible is God's words.

Giving God Thanks . . . a prayer to pray

One time I wanted all the ice cream I could eat. So I ate and ate till I felt sick, and couldn't take another lick! It wasn't very wise to want all the ice cream I could eat. But there is something wise to ask God for. We can ask for wisdom and God's help in being kind. Let's praise God for giving us wisdom with a fun rhyme.

I could ask to grow up tall,
(stretch up tall)
Or ask to shrink down very small.
(squat down)
I could ask for x-ray eyes,
(peek through your fingers)
But I'd rather ask to be kind and wise!
(give a hug)
Thank you, God, for helping me
Be wise and kind as I can be!
(jump with hands in the air)

Here are four things to ask of God above
to tell him our needs and show him our love.

I want to obey you, Lord, and always follow you.
I want to learn your Word that I know is true;
I want to make good choices, Lord, before your loving eyes.
I want to show the world your love,
so help me to be wise. Amen.

When we ask God to make us wise, it's a wise thing in God's sight—
Think of the ways God makes you wise as you fall asleep. Night-night!

Who heard and answered Daniel's prayers?
How many lions do you see?

Powerful Prayers

God said, "I will answer you." Jeremiah 33:3

Knowing God's Word . . . a story to read

Who's never too busy or makes us fuss, and takes the time to answer us? God! God hears our prayers, each and all, and always answers when we call! Daniel called upon God when the mean king wanted Daniel to pray to him instead of God.

Naughty, naughty! Mean King Darius was going to toss Daniel into a cave of lions! What do you think Daniel said? Daniel said, "Dear God, I'll only pray to you no matter what men say or do." Growly-scowly lions snarled at David as he prayed and asked God for help. And did God hear and answer Daniel? Yes he did! God answered Daniel on that growly night and closed the lions' jaws up tight! God hears and answers us, too. How do we know? The Bible tells us so.

GOD said, "I will answer U."

Jeremiah 33:3

Enjoying God's Gifts . . . a song to sing

I'm so happy! Can you guess why? I'm happy because God always has time for me. God always has time to hear me and answer me. He's never too busy to hear each little payer I pray, no matter if it's night or day! And God answers me in his time and way because he loves me! Just as God answered Daniel when he prayed, God answers our prayers, too. Let's sing God a happy song to thank him for taking the time to hear and answer us.

GOD WILL ANSWER
(tune: *Jesus Loves Me*)

**God will hear and answer us
Because he loves and cares for us—
God will answer in his way
When we bow our hearts to pray.
Yes, God will answer—
Yes, God will answer—
Yes, God will answer—
Because he loves us so.**

*Who is praying with Night-Light?
How many buttons can you count?*

Giving God Thanks . . . a prayer to pray

Sometimes my friends wonder why I pray. I tell them I want to talk to God each day to tell him I love him in every way. Let's thank God for answering us when we pray to him.

I don't care what the people say,
(shake your head and finger)
I want to pray to God each day!
(make prayer hands)
God will hear and answer me
(point upward)
'Cuz that's what God promises me!
(hand on heart)
I'll praise and honor God through prayer
(make prayer hands)
No matter when—no matter where!
(shake head and finger)
God will hear and answer me
(point upward)
'Cuz that's what God promises me!
(hand on heart)

Now here's a prayer for us to say to thank God for answering when we pray!

Dear God, you hear all that we say
When we bow our hearts to pray.
Thank you for answering in your way,
And for your loving help each day. Amen.

God always hears and answers us every day and night—
Think of how great God's answers are as you go to sleep. Night-night!

Who saved God's people by being brave?
Find the kitten and the necklace.

Be Brave!

God said, "Be strong and brave." Joshua 1:7

Knowing God's Word . . . a story to read

Sit up in bed. Now fall back onto your fluffy pillow. Were you scared? Not at all! You just knew you wouldn't fall! You were brave because you trusted your soft, cozy bed to catch you. We can trust God in much the same way. Because God is mightier than anything, we can trust in his power to save. And because we know God loves us so, through him we can be brave! Good Queen Esther was brave because she trusted God. When her people were in danger, Queen Esther trusted God. Through her courage, God's people were saved. Esther trusted God and was brave, and we can be brave, too.

God wants us to trust him and to be brave through his power. How do we know? The Bible tells us so!

GOD said, "strong and brave."

Joshua 1:7

Enjoying God's Gifts . . . a rhyme to say

Being brave is sometimes tough to do. Maybe you're afraid of lightning or the dark or even the goose at the beach by the park. But when we trust God and ask him to help us be brave, we can have special courage! Being brave comes from trusting God. And when we trust God, it's like giving God a special gift. Have Mommy or Daddy help you write the letters B-R-A-V-E on your left fingertips and the letters T-R-U-S-T on your right fingertips. Now you can spell the words "brave" and "trust" as we say this fun rhyme together.

B-R-A-V-E
(hold up each finger to spell "brave")
That's what God helps me to be!

T-R-U-S-T
(hold up each finger to spell "trust")
If I trust God faithfully!

Giving God Thanks . . . a prayer to pray

Good Queen Esther trusted God and was brave as she helped her people. Then what do you suppose Queen Esther did? She thanked God for making her brave. Let's praise and thank God for helping us to be brave. Say, "Thank you, God!" after each line.

For helping us trust your mighty power,
Thank you, God!
For staying beside us hour to hour,
Thank you, God!
For helping us be brave when we feel small,
Thank you, God!
For giving us courage so we feel tall,
Thank you, God!
We know you have the power to save,
Thank you, God!
And that through you we can be brave!
Thank you, God!

Now, let's share a prayer to thank God for helping us be brave.

Dear God, you have the power to save
And when we trust you, we'll be brave.
Please help us always turn to you
And stay brave and bold in all we do!
We love you! Amen.

God wants us to trust him and be brave with all our might—
Think of how God makes you brave as you go to sleep. Night-night!

What happened to Jonah when he tried to hide from God?
How many starfish do you see?

God Answers Us

God said, "I will answer you." Jeremiah 33:3

Knowing God's Word . . . a story to read

Cover your head with your pillow—oops! I can't see you! But there is someone who can! Who knows you're there and sees you all the time? God! God hears all we say and answers us in his own special way. Jonah tried to hide from God, but did it work? No siree! God saw Jonah and heard every word he prayed—even when the giant fish swallowed him! God heard Jonah say, "I'm sorry." God heard Jonah say, "Help me." And God answered Jonah's prayers as quickly as could be! Pfftooey! The fish spit Jonah on the sand and Jonah learned a giant lesson in the way God sees, and hears, and answers us.

God is always with us and hears each word we say. And because God loves us, he answers when we pray. How do we know? The Bible tells us so!

GOD said, "I will answer U."

Jeremiah 33:3

Enjoying God's Gifts . . . a song to sing

Jonah was being naughty when he tried to hide from God. He didn't deserve a special gift. But because Jonah told God he was sorry, and because God loved Jonah, God gave Jonah the gift of answering him. Every time God answers our prayers, it's like a special gift of love. God shows his love for us by listening to all we say and by answering every prayer we pray. We can give God a special thank-you gift by singing him a song. Fold your hands as if to pray and sing to God in a special way.

GOD WILL ANSWER
(tune: *Jesus Loves Me*)

**God will hear and answer us
Because he loves and cares for us—
God will answer in his way
When we bow our hearts to pray.
Yes, God will answer—
Yes, God will answer—
Yes, God will answer—
Because he loves us so.**

*Find the biggest fish that swallowed Jonah.
Point to the smallest fish, the striped fish,
the red fish, and the pink fish.*

Giving God Thanks . . . a prayer to pray

Sometimes when we call on the phone, we hear a busy sound—or the phone keeps ringing—ding-a-ling—because no one is around. I'm so glad that when we need to talk to God and have him answer us, he's always ready to listen. Let's praise and thank God for listening to us all and for answering us when we call.

I don't need a walkie-talkie,
(pretend to talk on a walkie-talkie)
I don't need to dial a phone;
(pretend to dial a telephone)
I don't need to type an e-mail,
(pretend to type a keyboard)
I don't need a microphone.
(pretend to hold a microphone)
When I want to talk with God, all I do is pray!
(make prayer hands)
And God will always answer me 24-hours a day! Yay!
(jump and cheer)

Let's share a prayer that God will hear because he loves us and he's near.

Dear God, I'm glad you always answer us
Because you love and care for us.
I'm glad you lend your loving ear
And that you answer because you're near.
I love you, God! Amen.

God always hears and answers us every day and night—
Think of how great God's answers are as you go to sleep. Night-night!

Remember to look
for my ladybug
friend in the Bible
story pictures!

What did baby Jesus sleep in the night he was born?
Name all the animals you can find.

Here and Near

God said, "I am with you." Jeremiah 30:11

Knowing God's Word . . . a story to read

God's love for you is bigger than the trees; it's taller than the mountains and wider than the seas. God loves you more than the stars or the sun, and to show you his love, he sent his precious Son! God loves us so much, he sent his Son Jesus so he could be with us all the time. God wanted to be near us, to help us and hear us. God wanted to be closer than a whisper to the ear, so he sent his Son Jesus to stay with us here. Jesus is with us all the time so we never have to feel alone or afraid. Isn't it great to have a friend like Jesus who's always right beside us?

God made a promise to always be with us. How do we know? The Bible tells us so!

GOD said, "I am with U."

Jeremiah 30:11

Enjoying God's Gifts . . . a rhyme to say

God has given us a special gift—the gift of Jesus and the gift of always being with us. God loves us and wants to be with us all the time, every hour of the day, come rain or shine. Isn't it a wonderful gift to know that the Lord is with us all the time, rain or shine? You can repeat this action rhyme and think about God's special gift of always being near.

Hickory, dickory, dock—
(make your arms "tick" like clock hands)

God is with me around the clock.
(make arm circles)

Rain or shine, all the time—
(make rain motions with your fingers, then put your hands over your head)

Hickory, dickory, dock!
(make your arms "tick" like clock hands again)

Tell about a time that God was with you. Thank God for being with you around the clock!

Giving God Thanks . . . a prayer to pray

Make a shadow on the wall. Can you make the shadow move up and down and dance around? Shadows seem to follow us wherever we go, but shadows stay with us only in the light. Jesus stays with us all the time, day or night, dark or light. Let's praise Jesus for being with us all the time by saying, "Thank you, Lord," after each line.

Jesus is with us; Jesus is here.
   Thank you, Lord.
Jesus will help us; Jesus is near.
   Thank you, Lord.
Jesus is mighty; Jesus is love.
   Thank you, Lord.
We praise you, Jesus, in heaven above!
   Thank you, Lord.

Here's a prayer for you to pray to thank our Creator for his loving way!

**Dear God, I'm glad you're with me night and day
And that Jesus stays beside me in sleep or play.
I know you're with me because you love me so,
Please stay beside me wherever I may go.
I love you, Lord! Amen.**

*God sent his Son Jesus to love us and be with us day and night—
Isn't it nice to know Jesus is with you as you fall asleep tonight?*

Whom did Jesus tell the temple teachers about?
Find three scrolls.

Love to Learn

Jesus said, "Learn from me." Matthew 11:29

Knowing God's Word . . . a story to read

Can you name these letters? J-E-S-U-S. Good for you!
Someone must have taught you these letters and you learned
them. You had a good teacher and you were a good learner. The
letters J-E-S-U-S spell the name of the best teacher we'll ever have.
Do you know what they spell? They spell Jesus' name! And Jesus
is our wonderful teacher. When Jesus was a young boy, he went
to the temple to learn about God and to teach others about him.

Jesus taught the teachers at the temple about God. The
teachers were amazed as they "oohed" and they "ahhed."
Imagine a young boy teaching so much about God! But Jesus
knew that people needed to learn about God from him. How do
we know? The Bible tells us so!

Jesus said, "Learn from me."

Matthew 11:29

Enjoying God's Gifts . . . a song to sing

I know a gift that's fun to receive in any kind of weather; it's a gift that never wears out and always lasts forever. What gift am I talking about? Why, the gift of learning that Jesus gives us! Jesus helps us learn important lessons that we can use to help us know God and get along with our family and friends. Every day with Jesus is like going to a wonderful school to learn! Oh, I don't want this class to ever end, do you? Let's thank Jesus for being the best teacher we have!

JESUS TEACHES
(tune: *The Alphabet Song*)

A-B-C-D-E-F-G—
Jesus teaches you and me.

He's our teacher and our friend—
I want his class to never end!

A-B-C-D-E-F-G—
Jesus teaches you and me.

How is Night-Light learning about God? Find the mouse.

Giving God Thanks . . . a prayer to pray

Think of all the things you've learned that help you as you live. You learned to talk and walk and skip; you've learned to be kind and to give. Maybe you've learned the alphabet or how to bat a ball. Now it's important for you to learn that Jesus is the best teacher of all! Let's praise and thank Jesus for teaching us. You can say, "We thank you, Jesus" after each line.

For teaching us that God is love,
We thank you, Jesus.
For helping us serve our Father above,
We thank you, Jesus.
For teaching us how to love one another,
We thank you, Jesus.
For helping us learn to forgive each other,
We thank you, Jesus.
For being the best teacher we ever will know,
We thank you, Jesus.
We praise you, Jesus, and love you so!
We thank you, Jesus.

Here's a prayer that we can pray to ask Jesus to teach us every day.

Dear Lord, we want to learn about you
So we will be wise in all that we do.
Please help us and teach us every day
In all that we do and each word we say. Amen.

Jesus teaches us lessons of love and how to treat others right—
Think of all that you have learned as you fall asleep. Good night!

What did Jesus do to obey God? Find the dove; count the balls.

Always Do Right

Jesus said, "Do all things that are right." Matthew 3:15

Knowing God's Word . . . a story to read

What makes Mommy happy? When you pick up all your toys. What makes Daddy happy? When you don't make too much noise. What makes Grandma happy? When you hug and kiss her tight. And what makes Jesus happy? When you try to do what's right! Jesus wants us to do good, kind things and to obey God. Jesus obeyed God when he was baptized. This was how Jesus told God he loved him. And God was happy that Jesus did what was right. Jesus always did what was good and right. And Jesus always obeyed God.

Jesus wants us to obey God, too. How do we know? The Bible tells us so!

JESUS said, "Do all things that R RIGHT."

Matthew 3:15

Enjoying God's Gifts . . . a song to sing

What did Jesus always do? Jesus always did what was right and he always obeyed God. Jesus gave God a gift of love when he obeyed. And when we obey God and do what's right, we show God we love him, too! When we do what's right in all that we do, what a nice way to say, "I love you!" Let's sing a fun song about obeying and saying, "I love you" to the Lord.

ALWAYS OBEY
(tune: *Three Blind Mice*)

Always obey! Always obey!
In all you do! And all you say!

Whenever we mind the way God wants us to,
And mind our Mommies and Daddies, too;

We'll bring smiles of love in all that we do—
Always obey! Always obey!

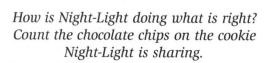

How is Night-Light doing what is right?
Count the chocolate chips on the cookie
Night-Light is sharing.

Giving God Thanks . . . a prayer to pray

I like to do right things and obey God, don't you? I know it's right to be kind and loving to one another. I know it's right to be forgiving of each other. And I know it's right to obey God in all we say and do. But it's not always easy. Isn't it good that Jesus helps us do what's right? Let's praise and thank Jesus for teaching us what's right so we can obey God in his sight!

No, not up,
> *(hop up)*

No, not down,
> *(squat down)*

No, not left,
> *(hop to the left)*

Or all around.
> *(turn around in a circle)*

Jesus helps us do what's right
> *(hop to the right)*

And we thank him with all our might!
> *(jump and point upward)*

Now here's a prayer for us to pray to ask Jesus to help us always obey.

Dear Lord, we want to do what's right
And obey you both day and night.
Please show us the things we ought to do
And ways to do what's right for you.
We love you, Lord! Amen.

Jesus always obeyed God and always did what's right—
Think of ways you can obey as you go to sleep. Night-night!

What were Peter and Andrew doing when they chose
to follow Jesus? Find the fishing boat and crab.

Follow-Me Fishermen

Jesus said, "Follow me." Matthew 4:19

Knowing God's Word . . . a story to read

March around the room to this rhyme: hop in the air, then clap one time. Stop your marching, turn around in place, now put a grin across your face. Clap three times, pat your head, hop two hops, then crawl in bed! You're good at following the leader because you listened to directions. Jesus wants us to follow him and listen to his directions, too. One day, Jesus met two brothers whose names were Peter and Andrew. Jesus invited these two fishermen to follow him. And what do you think they did? They followed! Peter and Andrew knew that Jesus would teach them about God and so they listened to Jesus' directions.

Jesus wants us to follow him, too. How do we know? The Bible tells us so!

Jesus said, "Follow Me."

Matthew 4:19

Enjoying God's Gifts . . . a song to sing

Weren't Peter and Andrew smart to follow Jesus? The two wise fishermen knew what to do; they followed Jesus—wouldn't you, too? Choosing to follow Jesus is a smart thing to do. Jesus is our perfect Leader and we can be his good followers. And when we choose to follow Jesus, we give him the gift of our love! What an important gift that is! We can sing a song you know. It's all about following the Leader we love and being led by him to our Father above!

FISHERS OF MEN
(traditional song)

I will make you fishers of men,
Fishers of men, fishers of men!
I will make you fishers of men
if you follow me!
If you follow me;
if you follow me—
I will make you fishers of men
if you follow me!

Find the matching pairs of fish.

Giving God Thanks . . . a prayer to pray

Cut out a paper fish and tape it to your shirt or hand. Now hop around your room and bend down to touch your toes. Climb back into bed, then put your finger on your nose. What did your fish do as you moved around? It followed you! We can follow Jesus too. Let's praise and thank Jesus for helping us be good followers. After each line, touch your paper fish and say, "I can follow, too!"

Jesus brings love to me and you.
I can follow, too!
Jesus was kind and helpful, too.
I can follow, too!
Jesus told others about God above,
I can follow, too!
And of our Father's forgiving love.
I can follow, too!
Jesus praised God's perfect name,
I can follow, too!
And teaches us to do the same!
I can follow, too!

Here's a prayer for me and you so we can tell Jesus we're his followers, too!

Dear Lord, you're our Leader perfect and true,
And we want to be your followers, too.
Please help us to follow in every way,
And to be like you in all we do and say. Amen.

Jesus wants us to follow him with all our love and might—
Think of how you can follow him as you drift to sleep. Night-night!

Who teaches us to love others no matter the person or place? Which of Night-Light's friends has an orange mane? A blue nose? A tall size?

Love Others

Jesus said, "Love each other." John 13:34

Knowing God's Word . . . a story to read

What do you look like? What color hair is on your head—is it blonde or black or brown or red? Are you slim, are you small, or do you stretch up long and tall? To Jesus, your looks don't matter at all! That's because Jesus loves each of us just the way we are. And Jesus wants us to love other people in the same way, too! We all live in different places; we have different thoughts and different faces. But Jesus loves us through and through and wants us to love others, too! I'm glad we're to love other people no matter the person or place; because when we show love to everyone, there's a smile on every face!

Jesus teaches us about being kind and loving to other people. How do we know? The Bible tells us so!

John 13:34

Enjoying God's Gifts . . . a song to sing

What happens when you show love to other people? People get happy even if they were sad; people get nice even if they were bad; people learn about their Father in heaven above when you share with them the gift of Jesus' love! Sharing the gift of your love with other people is such a happy thing! One smile leads to another and another and another . . . and pretty soon, there are smiles everywhere! Now wouldn't that be a wonderful sight? Here's a lively song we can sing to remind us that loving others is a wonderful thing!

THE KINDNESS SONG
(tune: *Ten Little Indians*)

Be kind and loving to one another,
Be forgiving of each other—
Show your love in all you do
'Cuz that's how God loves you!

How many smiles do you see? Name all the colors.

Giving God Thanks . . . a prayer to pray

Draw happy faces on the fingertips of both your hands. Can you count how many happy faces there are? Jesus wants us to love this many people and lots, lots more! Here's a fun finger rhyme for you to say to remind you to love other people each day!

Not just one person
(hold up one fingertip face)
Not just two
(hold up a second fingertip face)
Or even three or four—
(hold up two more faces)
Jesus says to show our love
To many, many more!
(wave all your fingertip faces)
Short or tall
(hold the faces low, then high)
Big or small
(stretch fingers out, then curl them in)
Jesus helps us love them all!
(wave all your fingertip faces)

Now here's a prayer for us to pray to show others our love each and every day.

Dear Lord, it's so nice to know
You love us through and through—
Please help us show our love and care
To other people, too! Amen.

Jesus wants us to love other people and help them smile bright—
Think of others you can love as you go to sleep. Good night!

What did Jesus do when the disciples were afraid?
Count the lightning bolts. Find the red belt.

Have No Fear!

Jesus said, "Don't be afraid." Matthew 10:31

Knowing God's Word . . . a story to read

What are you afraid of? Could it be spiders that cause you to shake or is it the dark that makes you quake? Jesus' friends were afraid one dark, stormy night. They were sailing along so peacefully when a storm came upon them suddenly. They thought the boat would sink down, down, down, and that they just might drown, drown, drown. But, who was with them in the boat and had the power to keep them afloat? Jesus was there! Jesus stopped the storm and calmed the waves and his disciples were no longer afraid.

Once I was afraid of ladybugs—they really gave me fear! I told Jesus and he took my fears away. Jesus wants us to trust him and not to be afraid. How do we know? The Bible tells us so!

Jesus said, "Don't bee afraid."

Matthew 10:31

Enjoying God's Gifts . . . a rhyme to say

Jesus didn't want his friends on the boat to be afraid. And Jesus doesn't want us to be afraid either. When we trust Jesus to help us and ask him to take away our fears, he does! Jesus is bigger than everything, so we're not afraid of anything. Let's enjoy this fun rhyme about not being afraid.

Thunder—pfoo!
(wrinkle your nose)
Lightning, too!
(wrinkle your nose)
I am not afraid of you!
(shake your head)
Spiders—pfoo!
(wrinkle your nose)
Darkness, too!
(wrinkle your nose)
I am not afraid of you!
(shake your head)
I won't shiver and I won't shake;
(shake your head)
I'll be brave for Jesus' sake.
(waggle your finger)
Jesus is bigger than any fear,
(hold arms over your head)
And I know that he's always here!
(give a thumbs-up sign)

How many spots are on the butterfly? Find the ladybug.

Giving God Thanks . . . a prayer to pray

God made ladybugs just as he made you and me! Jesus reminded me that God made the world and all that's in it—and that he's with us every minute! We can praise and thank Jesus for taking away our fears so we won't be afraid and so we can feel good about all God has made. You can say, "I thank you, Lord" after each phrase.

For being with us night and day,
I thank you, Lord.
For taking every fear away,
I thank you, Lord.
For your strength and perfect power,
I thank you, Lord.
For helping us through every hour,
I thank you, Lord.
For being bigger than any fear,
I thank you, Lord.
I love you, Lord, and hold you dear!
I thank you, Lord.

Now here's a prayer for us to pray to thank Jesus for taking our fears away.

Dear Lord, sometimes we feel afraid
And need a loving touch.
We're thankful you are with us
And that you love us so very much!
We love you, too, Lord. Amen.

Jesus wants us to trust him and not feel any fright—
Now let Jesus calm your fears as you go to sleep. Night-night!

What was in the boy's lunch that Jesus turned into enough to feed 5,000 people? Find the cucumber pie, a salad, a hotdog, ketchup, and a fork.

Heart Full of Help

Jesus said, "Help other people freely." Matthew 10:8

Knowing God's Word . . . a story to read

My tummy hurts! I feel like moaning. When I'm too full, my tummy starts groaning. I gobbled a hotdog and salad, too, with lots of seeds and dressing and goo. I munched a mound of cucumber pie that was topped with whipped cream a mile high! I wish I had shared my dinner. Jesus shared a meal with many hungry people. There were 5,000 tummies rumbling and growling. But there was only one small boy with one basket of food. How could five small fish and two loaves of bread feed such a hungry brood? Jesus blessed the boy's offering of help and the small bit of food became a feast of love!

Jesus wants us to help others, too! How do we know? The Bible tells us so!

JESUS said, "Help other freely."

Matthew 10:8

Enjoying God's Gifts . . . a song to sing

When you're hurting because you scraped your knee, what's the best gift there could be? A bandage, a kiss, and an "All better, see?" When we help others, it's like giving them a gift. And when we help others, we give a gift of love to Jesus, too! Here's a song to sing about helping one another!

DID YOU EVER HELP ANOTHER?
(tune: *Did You Ever See a Lassie?*)

Did you ever help another—
Your sister or brother?
Did you ever help another
with your loving heart?
Through kindness and caring
And sweet words and sharing—
Did you ever help another
with your loving heart?

Did you ever help another—
Your daddy or mother?
Did you ever help another
with your loving heart?
By washing the dishes
Or your hugs and kisses—
Did you ever help another
with your loving heart?

How is Night-Light helping his friend?

Giving God Thanks . . . a prayer to pray

A cookie is yummy when there's only one. But sharing a cookie is even more fun! Break a cookie in half and share it as you read this rhyme. Praise and thank Jesus for helping you care and share with others.

A piece for you and a piece for me
(share the cookie pieces)
Helps share the fun deliciously!
(give high fives)
Don't keep the fun inside of you—
(waggle your finger)
Care and share with others, too!
(give high fives)
We can help others and do our parts,
(point to someone else)
By helping and healing with love in our hearts!
(point to yourself)

Here's a prayer for us to pray to ask Jesus to help us help others every day.

Dear Lord, you help us all of our days
And show us your love in millions of ways.
Please help us find ways to help others, too,
And show them our lovingkindness, too. Amen.

Jesus wants us to help others with all of our might—
Think of ways to help others as you go to sleep. Good night!

Who stopped to help the man who was hurt in Jesus' story?
Now find the bandage, the skunk, a rose, and clover.

Kindness Counts!

Jesus said, "Show mercy." Luke 6:36

Knowing God's Word . . . a story to read

Once I helped a little skunk that no one wanted to; I pulled a splinter off his nose and then he sneezed, "ahh-choo!" I helped him out because I care like Jesus wants me to! Jesus wants us to show mercy and kindness to others—even people no one else will help! Jesus told a story about a man who lay hurt in the road. Poor man! He needed help in a terrible way, but only one man stopped to help that day. A man on a donkey came riding by, clip-clip-clop. And because that man had love in his heart, he decided to help and stopped. The Good Samaritan on the donkey helped the hurt man and showed him kindness and mercy.

Jesus wants us to show we care and help when someone needs us there. How do we know? The Bible tells us so!

Jesus said,

"Show mercy."

Luke 6:36

Enjoying God's Gifts . . . a game to play

Up rode the Good Samaritan, with clippity-clippy-clops. Down hopped the Good Samaritan; kindness never stops! What a gift of love the Good Samaritan gave the hurt man. We can give the gift of love by helping others, too. Here's a fun game to remind you how good it is to help others. Hop on your pillow donkey and clippity-clippy-clop; and you will always remember that kindness never stops!

Trot-trot, clip-clop
(ride your pillow)
Love and kindness never stop!
(pat your heart)
Jesus teaches us the way
(point upward)
To offer kindness every day!
(give the air a victory punch)

If someone needs your help today,
Trot right up, then smile and say,
"Jesus sent me to help you,
And that's just what I'm going to do!"

Trot-trot, clip-clop
(ride your pillow)
Love and kindness never stop!
(pat your heart)
Jesus teaches us the way
(point upward)
To offer kindness every day!
(give the air a victory punch)

What kind thing can you do for someone who needs help?

Giving God Thanks . . . a prayer to pray

How do you show others you'll help when they need you there? Is it through the words you share? Jesus spent his whole life being merciful and kind to others. We can, too! Let's praise and thank Jesus for helping us show mercy and kindness to others. After each line, you can say, "We thank you, Lord."

For giving us kind words to say,
We thank you, Lord.
For showing us your loving ways,
We thank you, Lord.
For guiding us to be wise and strong,
We thank you, Lord.
In helping others who come along;
We thank you, Lord.
For giving us tender hearts that care,
We thank you, Lord.
So we can help others who need us there,
We thank you, Lord.
We praise your loving name!
We thank you, Lord.

Here's a prayer for us to say to be kind and helpful every day.

Dear Lord, I'm glad you teach us the way
To be kind and merciful every day.
Help us help others who need us there,
And show them there's someone who really cares. Amen.

Jesus wants us to show mercy and kindness and we know that's right—
Think of how you can be kind to others as you fall asleep. Night-night!

What happened to the house that was built on a rock?
How many yellow bricks do you see? Find the hammer.

Building Trust

Jesus said, "Trust in me." John 14:1

Knowing God's Word . . . a story to read

Let's play a building game! Place two pillows on the floor
and stand on them. Ooo, don't wobble! Now stand on the floor.
You're standing so straight and solid! If you built a house on pillow
or on solid rock, which would be strongest? The house on the
rock, of course! Jesus told a story about two men who built
houses. One man was foolish and built his house on the sand.
What happened when the rains came and wouldn't stop? The sand
washed away and the house fell, kerplop! The wise man built his
house on solid ground. What happened when the rains came and
wouldn't stop? The house stood firm because it was built on rock!

How do you build a house? With a hammer and nails and
cement in pails. How do you build your life in Jesus? By trusting
him! How do we know? The Bible tells us so!

John 14:1

Enjoying God's Gifts . . . a song to sing

When we trust Jesus and have faith in his power to teach us and help us, we build strong lives in him. When we trust in Jesus we can stand strong when worries and troubles in life come along. Let's sing a fun song to remind us how important and wise it is to trust in Jesus.

THE RAINS CAME DOWN, THE FLOODS CAME UP

The foolish man built his house upon the sand;
The foolish man built his house upon the sand;
The foolish man built his house upon the sand;
    And the rains came tumbling down!
The rains came down and the floods came up;
The rains came down and the floods came up;
The rains came down and the floods came up;
    And the house on the sand washed away!

The wise man built his house upon the rock;
The wise man built his house upon the rock;
The wise man built his house upon the rock;
    And the rains came tumbling down!
The rains came down and the floods came up;
The rains came down and the floods came up;
The rains came down and the floods came up;
    But the house on the rock stood firm!

What tools is Night-Light using to build his house? Who will live in the house?

Giving God Thanks . . . a prayer to pray

The wise man built his house on the rock because rock is sturdy and strong, and he knew that sand doesn't last very long! It's the same when we build our lives on the rock-solid love of Jesus. Trusting Jesus makes us strong, and our faith in him lasts ever so long! Let's praise and thank Jesus with this fun rhyme.

Pound, pound, pound
(pound your fists together)
With a hammer swinging high—
That's the way we build a house
(put your arms over your head)
So we can live inside.

Thump, thump, thump
(pat your heart)
With a heart of trust and love—
That's the way we build our lives
(point to yourself)
In Jesus up above!
(point upward)

Now here's a prayer for you to pray to remind you to trust Jesus every day.

Dear Lord, I want to build my life in you
And trust you more in all I do.
Please help me always be more willing
To make you the rock on which I'm building! Amen.

Jesus wants us to trust him and hold onto him so tight—
Now think of how you trust Jesus as you go to sleep. Good night!

What did the shepherd do when one of his sheep was lost? Can you help him find his lost sheep? Find the sheep with the red bow.

Lost and Found

Jesus said, "I will be with you always." Matthew 28:20

Knowing God's Word . . . a story to read

How many sheep can you count with me? One sheep, 2 sheep, look, there's 3! 4, 5, 6 sheep—7, 8, 9 . . . Each sheep is precious and fluffy-fine! Jesus told a story about a shepherd with 100 sheep. The shepherd loved all his sheep, so when one sheep became lost, the shepherd searched. He looked up and down and all around 'til his fluffy sheep was finally found. The shepherd loved that lamb and wanted it close.

That's just how Jesus loves us. Even though there are many people Jesus loves, he loves each of us in a special way and wants us close to him. And because Jesus loves us so much, he's with us all the time! How do we know? The Bible tells us so!

JESUS said, "I will be with U always."

Matthew 28:20

Enjoying God's Gifts . . . a rhyme to say

It's wonderful to know that Jesus is always with us, isn't it? Just as glue binds and sticks things together, we're stuck like glue to Jesus and he's stuck to us with love! Here's a fun rhyme for you to say to remind you that Jesus is with you each day!

Stuck like glue, stuck like glue—
Jesus' love is stuck to you!
It can't come loose or melt away
'Cuz Jesus' love is here to stay!

Stuck like glue, stuck like glue—
We want to be stuck to Jesus, too!
We can love him every day
And say, "I love you!" when we pray!

Jesus is with me wherever I go—
When I walk in the sunshine or play in the snow.
He goes with me when I ride my bike,
Or swim in a pool, or go for a hike.
Name some other places Jesus goes with you.

Giving God Thanks . . . a prayer to pray

Give someone you love a kiss if he's near, and tell that someone you're glad he's here. Isn't it nice to be with the people you love? I like being with Teddy and all my other friends. I want to stay with them because I love them. Jesus wants to stay with us because he loves us, too. Let's praise and thank Jesus for being with us all the time.

For being with us when we're up or down;
(stretch up, then squat down)
For holding us when we're lost, then found;
(hide your eyes, then open them wide)
For staying close to us day or night;
(pretend to sleep)
For loving us with all your might;
(hug yourself)
For wanting us near as a heartbeat to you;
(pat your heart)
We praise you, dear Jesus, and thank you, too!
(blow a kiss upward)

Here's a prayer for you to pray to thank Jesus for staying beside you each day.

Dear Lord, I am so glad you're here
And that you always want me near.
You stay beside me, this I know,
And it's because you love me so.
I love you, too! Amen.

Jesus is with us all the time, every day and night—
Can you feel Jesus hugging you as you go to sleep? Good night!

Who helped the lame man so that he could walk again?
What colors are in the man's robe? Find four hearts.

Trust in Jesus

Jesus said, "Trust in me." John 14:1

Knowing God's Word . . . a story to read

When you ask Grandma for a drink that's cool, you trust that she will give it to you. How do you know that she'll give you a drink? Because Grandma loves you even more than you think! Trust is knowing someone loves you and will help you.

Long ago there was a man who couldn't walk. The man's friends trusted Jesus because they knew of his love. The men asked Jesus to help their friend and what do you think Jesus did? He used his power to fix the man's legs! Because his friends trusted Jesus, the man could walk and jump and leap for joy— boy oh boy! We can trust Jesus to help us, too! How do we know? The Bible tells us so!

John 14:1

Enjoying God's Gifts . . . a song to sing

What a special gift it is to be able to trust Jesus! When we trust Jesus, we know he will do everything he promises, like love us and help us, just as he helped the crippled man walk. We trust God and his Son Jesus with all our lives. Can you find the gift with the word "trust" on it? Trusting God and Jesus are gifts we give them that show our love. Let's give Jesus another gift! We can sing a song about trusting. You can point to the letters in the word "trust" as we sing.

TRUST
(tune: *Bingo*)

We always know what God will do
Because he tells us and it's true—

T-R-U-S-T
T-R-U-S-T
T-R-U-S-T

Have trust,
you really must!

The word "trust" begins with the letter "T". What other things in the picture begin with the letter "T"?

Giving God Thanks . . . a prayer to pray

When you hop into your cozy bed, you trust there's a pillow for your sleepy head. And when you get ready to dream away, you can trust that Jesus beside you will stay! We can trust Jesus to love us and help us and always stay with us. Let's praise and thank Jesus as we learn why we can trust him. You can say, "We thank you, Lord" after each phrase.

Because of the love you always give,
We thank you, Lord.
Because of your power to help us live,
We thank you, Lord.
Because of the truth you teach us each day,
We thank you, Lord.
Because you stay with us at work or at play,
We thank you, Lord.
Because you hear each and every prayer,
We thank you, Lord.
Because your forgiveness shows you care,
We thank you, Lord.

Here's a prayer for us to pray so we can trust Jesus more each day.

Dear Lord, it's so sweet to trust in you—
Whatever we say and whatever we do.
And when we have troubles and worries, too,
Please help us place our trust in you! Amen.

Jesus wants us to trust him with our hearts and all our might—
Think of ways you trust Jesus as you fall asleep. Night-night!

What did Jesus say about the children?
Find the freckles, the red hair, and the kitty.

Jesus Loves Kids!

Jesus said, "Come to me." Matthew 19:14

Knowing God's Word . . . a story to read

How old are you? What color is your hair? Do you have freckles on your nose or are they barely there? Is your name Martha or Emily or Jim? It doesn't matter who you are—Jesus wants you to come to him! Jesus loves everyone, but he especially loves children just like you! Once when Jesus was teaching a crowd of people, children came to him. Some of the people worried that Jesus wouldn't want kids around. Do you know what Jesus said? Jesus said, "Come to me! Let the little children come!" Jesus wants kids all around because he loves them—every one!

Sometimes grown ups want to be alone and they shoo us away. I'm so glad that Jesus wants us close to him each day! How do we know? The Bible tells us so!

Jesus said, "Come 2 me."

Matthew 19:14

Enjoying God's Gifts . . . a song to sing

What's the greatest gift we can give to Jesus from the start? The greatest gift Jesus wants to have is the gift of a child's heart! Jesus wants us to know and love him as much as he loves us. That's why Jesus wants us to come to him. I want to come to Jesus and stay with him in every way; I want to give my love to him and praise Jesus every day! Let's sing a new song to Jesus to tell him we love him and want to be near.

COME TO ME
(tune: *Deck the Halls*)

Jesus says, "Now come to me!"
Falalalala—lala—la—la!
That's just where I want to be—
Falalalala—lala—la—la!

Jesus' love will set us free—
Falala—falala—la—la—la!
Jesus loves us all you see!
Falalalala—lala—la—la!

Jesus wants all children to be close to him.
How many children are in this picture?

Giving God Thanks . . . a prayer to pray

Jesus wants us near him so we can learn what he teaches and feel his love and so we can know our Father above. When we learn about Jesus and read the Bible and pray, we move closer to Jesus in every way. Let's praise and thank Jesus for wanting us near him. Follow along as we move closer to Jesus. Each time you move, you can say, "Jesus says, 'Come to me!'"

Take two steps forward as quick as quick can be—
Jesus says, "Come to me!"
Take three steps slowly—1, 2, 3—
Jesus says, "Come to me!"
Take a giant hop forward, then you'll see—
Jesus says, "Come to me!"
Take three steps forward on your knee—
Jesus says, "Come to me!"
Now praise Jesus with a heart that's free!
Yippee!

Let's say a prayer to thank Jesus for loving kids everywhere and wanting us all to be so near.

Dear Jesus, I'm so glad
That you love kids and tots;
And that you want us near
Because you love us lots.
We love you, too, Jesus! Amen.

Jesus wants us close to him to love us sweet and tight—
Think of how Jesus loves you as you go to sleep. Night-night!

Who did Zacchaeus want to see when he climbed up in
that very tall tree? Find the coin bag and count the coins.

Forgiven for Love

Jesus said, "Forgive other people." Luke 6:37

Knowing God's Word . . . a story to read

Have you ever forgiven someone? It feels nice to forgive others and it makes them feel good, too. That's why Jesus wants us to forgive people when they say or do wrong things. Do you remember the funny guy named Zacchaeus, who wasn't very tall? He was a greedy tax collector who was mean to one and all. He treated people unkindly each day that he was living—and even though Zacchaeus was awful, Jesus was forgiving! Jesus forgave Zacchaeus and guess what happened then? Zacchaeus liked the people and was nice to all of them!

So if my friend steps on my shoe, I'll say, "Don't worry! I forgive you." That's what we're supposed to do! How do we know? The Bible tells us so!

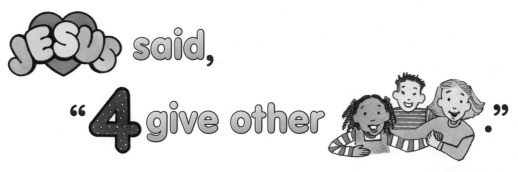

Jesus said, "**4**give other ."

Luke 6:37

Enjoying God's Gifts . . . a song to sing

When you say or do something you didn't mean to, what's the best gift someone can give to you? The gift of forgiveness! When we offer someone our forgiveness, we also give them the gifts of love, kindness, and understanding. We all make mistakes, it is true—so you can forgive me and I'll forgive you! And the best part? Jesus will forgive us, too! Let's sing a song you already know about being kind and forgiving to one another.

THE KINDNESS SONG
(tune: *Ten Little Indians*)

**Be kind and loving to one another,
Be forgiving of each other—**

**Show your love in all you do
'Cuz that's how God loves you!**

*Oh-oh! What will Night-Light need to
ask Teddy to do? How can you be
kind like Night-Light and Teddy?*

Giving God Thanks . . . a prayer to pray

Zacchaeus changed from a mean guy to a nice guy when Jesus forgave him. When we forgive other people, they change, too. Let's praise and thank Jesus for forgiveness. Give a "thumbs down" if the phrase is about being mean, and a "thumbs up" if the phrase is about forgiving others.

If someone calls me a mean, nasty name,
(thumbs down)
I will forgive them and not do the same!
(thumbs up)
If other kids bop me or push me around,
(thumbs down)
I will forgive them and not push them down!
(thumbs up)
I'll praise Jesus, for I know that it's true,
(thumbs up)
"If you forgive others who aren't nice to you—
(thumbs down)
Our loving Lord will forgive you, too!"
(thumbs up)

Here's a prayer for us to pray to be more forgiving every day.

Dear Lord, you love us each day that we're living,
Please help us be loving and always forgiving.
Just as you forgive for the wrong things we do,
Please help us forgive in the same way, too. Amen

Jesus wants us to forgive other people and make their hearts light—
Think of how good forgiveness feels as you go to sleep. Good night!

How many coins did the woman give to God? Why was God happy with her gift? Find the striped robe.

Good Giving

Jesus said, "Give to God." Matthew 22:21

Knowing God's Word . . . a story to read

What's the most special gift you've given to someone? Was it a flower or a book like this? A picture you drew or a simple kiss? Whatever your gift, you probably gave it with great love. A woman in the Bible gave a great gift to God. Jesus told how the woman gave the only thing she had. Did she give God goats or a pair of mules? Did she offer him gold or diamonds and jewels? No, the woman gave God her two copper coins. Those coins weren't shiny, they were really quite small, but God loved her gift because she gave her all! The two coins were all the woman had to give—and she gave them cheerfully to God.

Jesus wants us to give to God like the woman who gave her two coins cheerfully. How do we know? The Bible tells us so!

JESUS said, "Give 2 GOD."

Matthew 22:21

Enjoying God's Gifts . . . a game to play

Cut out two big circle coins from brown paper bags. Draw stars or a moon on one paper coin and a happy sun on the other. Your paper coins can help you give to God just as the old woman gave to God. Each morning, place your happy sun on your pillow and tell God you love him. And each night, place the nighttime coin on your pillow and give God your prayers. Here's what you can say:

Good morning, God, good morning to you—
Today I'll give all my love to you!

Good night, God, I'm glad you're there—
Now I want to give you a special prayer!

Giving God Thanks . . . a prayer to pray

Think of all the things God gives to you—a family to love and good food to eat, too. God gives the sunshine to help flowers grow, and sends delights like bright stars and snow. What can you give to God? You can give him your prayers, you can give God your love; you can give praise and thank-yous to our Father above. After each sentence, you can say, "Thank you, Lord."

May we always give our love to you
And show others kindness in all that we do.
  Thank you, Lord.
May we give you our prayers each day and night
And trust in your answers to make things all right.
  Thank you, Lord.
May we always give our hearts to you
And see the great things that you always do.
  Thank you, Lord.
May we always give from our blessings and love
And return them to you, our Father above!
  Thank you, Lord.

Here's a prayer that we can pray to give the Lord our love today!

Dear Lord, you bless us in every way
And we want to give to you each day.
We want to give our love to you
And live our lives as gifts to you! Amen.

Jesus wants us to give love to God with all our might—
Tell God how you love him as you go to sleep. Good night!

How did the people welcome Jesus when he came to town?
Find these colored robes: yellow, purple, blue, pink, orange.

Welcome, Jesus!

Jesus said, "Be ready!" Luke 12:40

Knowing God's Word . . . a story to read

Do you have a "Welcome" mat outside your door? Welcome mats are used near doors to greet people when they come to see you. It's nice to give others a warm welcome, isn't it? Long ago, Jesus was going to visit the town of Jerusalem. What do you think the people did? They got all ready for Jesus to come and planned a very warm welcome. The people placed their robes on the ground and Jesus rode over them on his way to town. The people waved palm branches in the air to show Jesus they were glad that he was there. What a welcome was ready and waiting for Jesus!

When we get ready for Jesus, we put love in our hearts, read God's Word, and obey all God says. Jesus wants us to be ready for him! How do we know? The Bible tells us so!

Enjoying God's Gifts . . . a rhyme to say

It's fun to get ready to welcome Jesus, isn't it? We want to welcome Jesus every day and tell him we love him. When we do, it's a wonderful gift we give Jesus! Think about the word "welcome." It sounds like there are two words in "welcome," doesn't it? There's "well" and "come." Let's use the words "well" and "come" to welcome Jesus into our hearts and tell him we love him.

Well come, Jesus,
(motion as if saying, "come here")
into my heart—
(pat your heart)
I want to welcome you right from the start!
(hop in the air)
I want you beside me
(pat your side)
Each day and each night,
(pretend to sleep)
I want to obey you
(point upward)
And always do right.
(nod your head)
Well come, Jesus,
(motion as if saying, "come here")
into my heart—
(pat your heart)
I want to welcome you right from the start!
(hop in the air)

Can you name the letters on the welcome mat?

Giving God Thanks . . . a prayer to pray

Cut out a big paper leaf. Can you wave your leaf back and forth? This is what the people did to welcome Jesus into their city. We want to welcome Jesus into our hearts and lives. How do we welcome him? We welcome Jesus with the love and trust our hearts can raise, and we welcome Jesus with our thanks and praise! Let's praise Jesus as we welcome him to our lives. You can wave your paper leaf when you hear the word "hosanna."

Hosanna, hosanna—get ready for Jesus!
For he is the one who loves and frees us!

Hosanna, hosanna—our hearts are raised,
For Jesus is Lord and greatly to be praised!

Hosanna, hosanna—let's welcome our Jesus,
For he is the one who loves and frees us!

Here's a prayer for us to pray to get ready for Jesus right away.

Dear Lord, make our hearts ready so you will know
How welcome you are and how we love you so!
We want you in our lives in every way
To love us and guide every day!
We love you, Jesus! Amen.

Jesus wants us to be ready to love him tight—
Think of how you love Jesus as you go to sleep. Good night!

How did Jesus serve his friends after their dinner? Find the red chair, a towel, a pan of water, and a pair of sandals.

Serve Like Jesus

Jesus said, "Be like the servant." Luke 22:26

Knowing God's Word . . . a story to read

How do you get ready for supper? You set the table so it looks nice—you fill the glasses with water, then add the ice. You serve up the food that you helped prepare—you say a blessing or thank-you prayer. Then you eat! Helping serve dinner to your family is fun. And Jesus wants us to be servants and helpers. Long ago, Jesus' friends fixed and shared a special supper with Jesus. Then Jesus taught them about being servants. After dinner, Jesus washed the feet of his friends. He washed their feet to show them that we must help and serve one another and be kind and loving to each other.

Friends and family, sister, brother—
Jesus said to serve each other!

How do we know? The Bible tells us so!

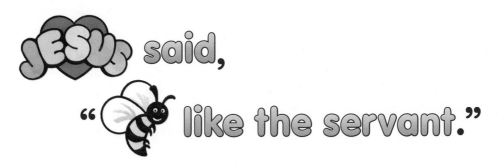

Jesus said, "Be like the servant."

Luke 22:26

Enjoying God's Gifts . . . a song to sing

Jesus wants us to serve one another and be kind and helpful to each other. That's because Jesus knows that being like servants shows other people we care and want to see them happy. When we help others, it's like giving them a gift of love. And when we serve others, we give that gift of love to Jesus, too! Here's a song to remind us about serving one another!

DID YOU EVER HELP ANOTHER?
(tune: *Did You Ever See a Lassie?*)

Did you ever help another—
Your sister or brother?
Did you ever help another
with your loving heart?
Through kindness and caring
And sweet words and sharing—
Did you ever help another
with your loving heart?

Did you ever help another—
Your daddy or mother?
Did you ever help another
with your loving heart?
By washing the dishes
Or your hugs and kisses—
Did you ever help another
with your loving heart?

How is Night-Light serving his friend?

Giving God Thanks . . . a prayer to pray

Find a plate you can pass back and forth. Hand the plate to someone and say, "With love I'll serve you, because Jesus wants me to." Jesus didn't just tell us how to serve others—he showed us! Let's praise and thank Jesus by passing the plate each time you hear the word "serve."

Serve up a little kindness,
Serve each other happily—
When we're like a servant,
We're like we're supposed to be!

Serve up a heap of help,
Serve without a fuss—
When we're like a servant,
Jesus smiles on us!

Serve up a little patience,
Serve up a lot of love—
When we're like a servant,
We serve our Lord above!

Here's a prayer for us to pray to ask Jesus' help in serving the right way.

Dear Lord, we want to serve each other
And be helpful and kind to one another.
Please show us how to serve in different ways
So we can be servants all of our days. Amen.

Jesus wants us to be like servants each day and night—
Think of ways you can serve others as you fall asleep. Sleep tight!

What did Jesus do to show his love for you and me?
Find the flower and the butterfly.

Forgiven With Love

Jesus said, "Forgive them." Luke 23:34

Knowing God's Word . . . a story to read

*The saddest day there has ever been
Was when Jesus died to forgive our sins.
But the happiest times that come from livin'
Are when we forgive others as we've been forgiven!*

Do you know how much Jesus loves you? Jesus loves you so much that he stays with you all the time. Jesus loves you so much that he helps and cares for you every day. And Jesus loves you so much that he died to forgive all the wrong things you might say or do. Wow! That's a lot of love, isn't it? Jesus died to forgive our sins and to show us God's love never ends.

When we forgive as Jesus has done, then we bring God's love to everyone! How do we know? The Bible tells us so!

Jesus said, "4 give them."

Luke 23:34

Enjoying God's Gifts . . . a song to sing

Jesus gave us a precious gift when he chose to die for us. Jesus forgave us and showed us his love, so we could be friends with our Father above. When we forgive others, we give Jesus a gift of love, too! Let's sing Jesus a special song to express our love to him.

JESUS LOVES ME
(tune: *traditional*)

Jesus loves me this I know,
For the Bible tells me so—
Little ones to him belong,
They are weak but he is strong!
Yes, Jesus loves me!
Yes, Jesus loves me!
Yes, Jesus loves me! The Bible tells me so.

Jesus gave his life for us
Because he loves and cares for us—
We can say, "Lord, I love you,"
When we forgive our brothers, too.
Yes, Jesus loves me!
Yes, Jesus loves me!
Yes, Jesus loves me! The Bible tells me so.

Once, my friend broke my new kazoo,
But it wasn't on purpose—he didn't mean to.
I remembered how Jesus has forgiven me,
So I forgave my friend quite joyfully!

Giving God Thanks . . . a prayer to pray

Jesus forgave us because he loves us. And we can show love to others by forgiving them, too. Forgiving others allows good feelings to grow and it keeps people from being angry with each other. Let's praise and thank Jesus for showing us how to forgive each other. After each line, you can say, "We thank you."

For helping us learn about God above,
We thank you.
For showing us God's perfect love,
We thank you.
For giving your life for us,
We thank you.
For your love in forgiving us,
We thank you.
For taking on our awful sins—
We thank you.
And showing us God's love never ends,
We thank you.
We praise and thank you, Jesus!
We thank you.

Now here's a prayer for you to pray to thank Jesus for his love each day.

Dear Lord, I feel your love each day
And I'm glad you forgive me in every way.
Please help me be forgiving, too;
It's the best way to say, "I love you!" Amen.

Jesus wants us to forgive others and love them with all our might—
Think of how Jesus forgives and loves you as you go to sleep. Good night!

181

How did Jesus' friends feel when they found out he was alive?
How many happy faces can you count?

182

Jesus Is Alive!

Jesus said, "I will be with you always." Matthew 28:20

Knowing God's Word . . . a story to read

Jesus is alive today! We're so happy, shout "Hooray!"
Jesus is alive today—and forevermore!

That's the happy song Jesus' friends must have sung on the morning they knew Jesus was alive! Jesus had died to forgive our sins. Oh, how sad Jesus' friends were. Three days after Jesus died—1, 2, 3—Jesus' friends went to his tomb and bent to peek inside. What do you think they saw? Nothing! That's because Jesus was risen from death. And Jesus promises to be with us forever. Jesus' friends were so happy that they ran to tell the Good News!

Jesus promised that he will always be right beside both you and me! How do we know? The Bible tells us so.

JESUS said, "👁 will 🐝 with U always." Matthew 28:20

Enjoying God's Gifts . . . a song to sing

Good news always makes me so excited and happy. I just can't wait to share good news with others, can you? That's because good news is meant to be shared. Just as Jesus' friends shared the Good News about Jesus being alive, we can share that Good News, too! Who can you tell that Jesus is alive today and will be with us night and day? Let's sing a special song to celebrate the wonderful news that Jesus is alive! You can even make up more actions and verses on your own!

JESUS IS ALIVE TODAY
(tune: *London Bridge*)

**Jesus is alive today!
Clap your hands and shout "Hooray!"
Jesus is alive today, and forevermore!**

**Jesus is alive today!
Twirl around and shout "Hooray!"
Jesus is alive today, and forevermore!**

**Jesus is alive today!
Pat your toes and shout "Hooray!"
Jesus is alive today, and forevermore!**

*Night-Light is praising Jesus with
a song. Which instruments
can you name?*

Giving God Thanks . . . a prayer to pray

Just imagine the excitement and joy of that first Easter morning when Jesus' friends knew he was alive! I'm sure they couldn't keep their hearts and lips from singing praises to our Lord. We can praise and thank Jesus, too! After each line, clap your hands and say, "I'll clap my hands and praise you, Lord!"

Because I love and treasure you,
I'll clap my hands and praise you, Lord!
For all the wondrous things you do,
I'll clap my hands and praise you, Lord!
Because you gave your life for me,
I'll clap my hands and praise you, Lord!
Because you promise to stay with me,
I'll clap my hands and praise you, Lord!
For showing me the way to our Father above,
I'll clap my hands and praise you, Lord!
Because you're alive and you give me your love,
I'll clap my hands and praise you, Lord!

Now here's a prayer for you to pray to praise Jesus for being with us today.

Dear Lord, when you died for us we felt such sadness
But now there's only joy and gladness!
For you are Lord and we can say,
"We're so glad you're alive today!"
We love you, Jesus! Amen.

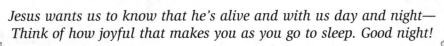

Jesus wants us to know that he's alive and with us day and night—
Think of how joyful that makes you as you go to sleep. Good night!

What did Jesus tell his friends to do? Help Night-Light find all his friends so he can tell them the Good News about Jesus!

Tell the Good News

Jesus said, "Tell the Good News." Mark 16:15

Knowing God's Word . . . a story to read

It's fun to tell exciting news, isn't it? And we have the best news of all. We can tell about Jesus and his love! Jesus told his friends to tell others about him and how he forgives us. Jesus told his friends to tell about how Jesus was risen from death and is alive. And Jesus told them to baptize others and help them trust in God. So Jesus' friends ran to share the Good News! They told their neighbors and their friends; they told how Jesus' love never ends. They told their fathers, sisters, and brothers; they shared the Good News with their Grandmas and mothers.

I think Jesus smiles when I tell the Good News, too, because that's just what he wants us to do! How do we know? The Bible tells us so!

Jesus said, "Tell the Good NEWS."

Mark 16:15

Enjoying God's Gifts . . . a rhyme to say

Find a sheet of newspaper and roll it up. Pretend to be a paperboy and hand the news to someone. Good for you! Every day paperboys put on their walkin' shoes to take other people the daily news. They walk and walk to deliver the news so others can learn from it. Now draw a cross on the newspaper to remind us of Jesus. Draw a happy face on the newspaper to show how it feels to love Jesus. Draw a heart shape on the newspaper to show how Jesus loves you. And draw big smiling lips on the paper to show how we can tell others about Jesus. Let's use your newspaper to say a rhyme about sharing the Good News about Jesus with others.

Jesus died and was risen for you;
(point to the cross)
That makes us happy and thankful, too!
(point to the happy face)
Jesus forgives us and shows us his love;
(point to the heart)
Now go and tell others of your Lord above!
(point to the smile)
Go ahead and put on your walkin' shoes
And deliver to others Jesus' Good News!
(give the newspaper to someone)

Who is Night-Light telling the Good News to?

Giving God Thanks . . . a prayer to pray

The very best news that I know, is all about how Jesus loves us so! Do you know what I like to do? I like to tell others, "Jesus loves you!" Everyone smiles when they hear good news! And telling someone about the way Jesus loves and forgives us is the best news we can share! Let's praise and thank Jesus for giving us such wonderful news to share. You can say, "We thank you, Jesus" after each line.

For giving us Good News to share,
We thank you, Jesus.
For showing us you always care,
We thank you, Jesus.
For helping us tell others about God above,
We thank you, Jesus.
For giving us forever life through your love,
We thank you, Jesus.
For helping us tell our friends about you—
We thank you, Jesus.
And all of the amazing things you can do,
We thank you, Jesus.

Now here's a prayer for us to pray to help us tell others about Jesus each day.

Dear Lord, I really love you so
And want the whole wide world to know!
Please help me tell my family and friends
About your love, which never ends. Amen.

Jesus wants us to tell others about his love pure and bright—
Think of what you can tell as you fall asleep. Good night!

What gift did Jesus send that came upon his friends with a whoosh like the wind? Find ten hearts.

Welcome, Holy Spirit!

Jesus said, "Receive the Holy Spirit." John 20:22

Knowing God's Word . . . a story to read

Jesus promised a present—what could it be?
Wrapped with ribbons for you and for me?
No, the gift that Jesus promised to send
Is a helper, a healer, a teacher, and friend!

What gift did Jesus give us? Jesus gave us the gift of the Holy Spirit! Before Jesus died for us, he promised to send us someone who would help us follow him. Jesus' friends were amazed when the Holy Spirit arrived with a whoosh like the wind. They knew someone special had come to love them as Jesus watched from heaven above them! The Holy Spirit is our helper and friend; he's the gift Jesus promised to send!

Jesus wants us to welcome the Holy Spirit into our lives. How do we know? The Bible tells us so!

 said,

"Receive the Holy Spirit."

John 20:22

Enjoying God's Gifts . . . a song to sing

I can't think of a better gift than the gift of a loving friend—
One who will always stay by me and feel the love I send.

Jesus sent the Holy Spirit to be our helper, teacher, and friend and we can warmly welcome him. So, let's welcome the Holy Spirit into our hearts and lives with a song and a cheer and let him know we're glad he's here!

THANK YOU FOR THE HOLY SPIRIT
(tune: *Hark! The Herald Angels Sing*)

Thank you, Lord, we know you'll hear it—
Thank you for the Holy Spirit!
He's the gift you promised to send;
He's our helper and our friend!

The Holy Spirit helps us do
All the things you want us to—
He's our friend so now let's hear it,
Let's give a welcome to the Holy Spirit!

He's our friend so now let's hear it,
Let's give a welcome to the Holy Spirit!
(Give a cheer and a "Welcome, Holy Spirit!")

What can we tell
the Holy Spirit?

Giving God Thanks . . . a prayer to pray

Sometimes my friends are busy and can't come over to play or help me clean house. But I know that my special friend, the Holy Spirit, is never too busy to be with me or help me! Let's praise and thank Jesus for sending us such a wonderful friend!

For promising that you would send
(point up, then down)
A perfect helper
(give a thumbs-up sign)
And loving friend—
(give yourself a hug)
To help us bravely say and do
(pat a fist over your heart)
All the things you want us to—
(point upward)
We give you thanks and know you'll hear it;
(cup hand to ear)
Thank you, Lord, for the Holy Spirit!
(jump with arm stretched up)

Now here's a prayer for us to pray to welcome the Holy Spirit in a special way.

Dear Lord, we're so very thankful you knew
That we'd need a helper who loves us like you.
Please help us to welcome the Holy Spirit
As we tell him we love him so he will hear it!
We love and thank you, too! Amen.

Jesus wants us to welcome the Holy Spirit with all our love and might—
Tell the Holy Spirit you're glad he's here as you go to sleep. Night-night!

What happened when Peter prayed while
he was in jail? Find the mouse.

Pray Each Day

Jesus said, "Ask and you will receive." John 16:24

Knowing God's Word . . . a story to read

Once I was lost in the grocery store. I was by the green beans and pears and couldn't find Mommy anywhere! I thought that I'd give God a prayer, but would he hear me even there? He did! Mommy found me and now I know that God will help me wherever I am if I just ask him.

Long ago, Peter found out that God hears and helps anywhere, too! Peter was in jail for telling others about Jesus. But Peter prayed and so did his friends. They asked God to help Peter, but Peter was in jail; would God help him even there? He did! God sent angels to free Peter so he could keep telling people about Jesus. Jesus wants us to ask God for his help. And Jesus knows that God will help when we ask him. How do we know? The Bible tells us so!

 said,

"Ask and U will receive."

John 16:24

Enjoying God's Gifts . . . a song to sing

God will always answer us and help us when we ask him! What a gift of love that is! It makes me feel good to know that God is never too busy to listen to me or answer me. Jesus promised that when we ask God for his help through prayer, we will receive his loving help—any time and anywhere! Just like Peter, we can trust God to help us when we ask him. Let's sing God a happy song to thank him for taking the time to hear and answer us.

GOD WILL ANSWER
(tune: *Jesus Loves Me*)

God will hear and answer us
Because he loves and cares for us—
God will answer in his way
When we bow our hearts to pray.
Yes, God will answer—
Yes, God will answer—
Yes, God will answer—
Because he loves us so.

*What does Night-Light remember
to do when he needs some help?*

Giving God Thanks . . . a prayer to pray

God knows when we need help even if we don't say so. But God wants us to ask him for help. God wants us to trust him and believe in his help. God likes it when we talk to him in prayer and he promises to help us anytime or anywhere! Let's praise and thank God for his help and love. You can help by using your words and your fingers as we say this rhyme.

One little prayer I say to God above.
(hold up one finger)
Two hands that clap when he answers me with love.
(clap your hands)
Three small words I'll say to God when I pray—
Please, help me!
Four words of thanks when he answers right away—
Thank you very much!
Five important words that we can always believe,
(hold up five fingers)
Were said to us by Jesus, "Ask and you will receive."

Now here's a prayer for us to pray to remember to ask God's help each day.

Dear Lord, we know that when we need help
All we have to do is pray,
And you will hear and answer us
Anytime night or day!
Thank you for loving us, Lord! Amen.

Jesus tells us that we can ask God for his help to make things right—
What can you ask God to help you with as you go to sleep? Good night!

Where is Jesus making a new home for us?
Find something purple, blue, orange, red, and pink.

New for You!

Jesus said, "I am making everything new!" Revelation 21:5

Knowing God's Word . . . a story to read

New things are nice, aren't they? Old shoes are worn and hurt your feet, while new shoes are a comfortable treat. Old cars are clinkety and might not run well, while new cars are shiny with that special new smell. Our old lives before we knew Jesus as our Savior and friend were sad, while our new lives in Jesus are shiny, loving, and glad! Jesus is making everything new for us. He is at work right now preparing a new home for us in heaven: a home filled with laughter, sunshine, and love; a new home in heaven with our Father above.

Jesus wants us to be done with the old and welcome the new—and he's making things beautiful and fresh just for you! How do we know? The Bible tells us so!

Jesus said, "I am making everything new."

Revelation 21:5

Enjoying God's Gifts . . . a rhyme to say

Look around and count the windows you see! One or 2 or even 3? There are many more windows in our heavenly home! Jesus promised it would be a mansion with plenty of room for everyone. Let's take time to imagine what our new heavenly home will be like someday. Draw a picture in your mind, and don't let it go away. Now think about your heavenly home as we say a special rhyme to help us remember that Jesus is making all things new because he loves and cares for us, too!

> **Just imagine our heavenly home—**
> **With so much space for us to roam!**
>
> **Golden doorknobs and windows with jewels—**
> **Nothing to break, so we won't need our tools!**
>
> **Just close your eyes and imagine a place**
> **Where God's glory and love lights up each face!**
>
> **We give thanks, dear Jesus, from us to you,**
> **For making our heavenly home fresh and new!**

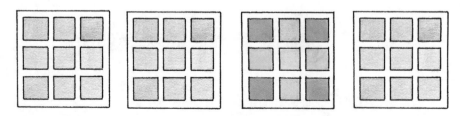

Point to the window that is different from all the others.

Giving God Thanks . . . a prayer to pray

Fold a piece of paper in half to make a card. Ask Mommy or Daddy to write "Thank You" on the front of your card. When do you give a thank-you card to someone you know? When that someone does something special for you and sets your heart aglow! It makes me feel happy to know that Jesus is making a new heaven and earth for us to someday enjoy. Let's give Jesus a special thank-you. After each phrase, hold up your thank-you card and say, "Jesus, I give my thanks to you!"

For the way you love and care for me, too—
Jesus, I give my thanks to you!
For making my heart feel shiny and new—
Jesus, I give my thanks to you!
For all the wonderful things you do—
Jesus, I give my thanks to you!
For making a new earth and heaven, too—
Jesus, I give my thanks to you!
I praise you, Jesus, and give my love to you!

Now here's a prayer for you to pray to thank Jesus for making everything new in his own special way.

Dear Lord, we thank you for all that you do,
And for the home you're making anew.
We're happy to someday live in heaven above,
And be there beside you to give you our love! Amen.

Jesus promises he is making everything new and bright—
Think of our heavenly home as you go to sleep. Night-night!

God bless you and good night!

Scripture Index

"God said" verses

"Jesus said" verses

Susan L. Lingo has spent most of her life working with and writing for children of all ages. A former early childhood and elementary school teacher, Susan is the author of over forty-five Christian books and resources for kids, teachers, and parents—including the bestselling Gold Medallion nominee, *My Good Night® Bible* and *My Good Night® Devotions*. Now Susan's lively approach and age-appropriate style come together again in *My Good Night® Prayers*. Using soothing rhythm and rhyme, Susan hopes to help busy parents and children share a peaceful, cozy time together and quiet times with God. Susan and her husband reside in Loveland, Colorado, with their two children, Lindsay and Dane. When she's not busy creating great projects as the owner and operator of Bright Ideas Books and Book Production, Susan enjoys her cats, tennis, golf, reading, and of course, working with children.

Kathy Parks first began drawing around age three, using leftover paper from her uncle's print shop. She has been a fashion illustrator, courtroom artist, commercial artist, and the illustrator of over 200 music lesson books. She has illustrated other books for Standard Publishing, including *My Good Night® Bible* and *My Good Night® Devotions*. Her delightful designs once again express the freedom found within the protective structure of God's grace. Kathy teaches Sunday school in San Diego, California, where she lives with her husband and their two children.

MY GOOD NIGHT® Snuggle-up FAVORITES

My Good Night® Bible (03623)

Forty-five Old and New Testament Bible stories will capture the heart and imagination of your preschooler, and become a favorite part of your bedtime routine. *My Good Night® Bible* was nominated for a 2000 ECPA Gold Medallion Award.

My Good Night® Devotions (04000)

In these multicultural stories based on biblical principles, Sam, Sophie, Max, Polly, Jimmy and Mia learn how God's Word works in their everyday lives. Children will discover how to make decisions and how to do the right thing, in this companion book to the best-selling *My Good Night® Bible.*

My Good Night® Christmas (03683)

Created by the same author-artist team who produced the best-selling *My Good Night® Bible!* The book and read-along CD feature six short stories that tell the Christmas story. Narrated by Nan Gurley, the CD also features the Wonder Kids Choir singing such favorites as "Away in a Manger," "Silent Night" and more.

My Good Night® Bible Songs (04008)

Your child will love to play songs like "Jesus Loves Me," "Zacchaeus," and "Hallelu, Hallelu" on easy-to-follow color-coded keys. Night-Light shares a thought about each Bible story, too.